YOU the Divine Genius

YOU are more than you think you are

This book is dedicated to:

the magical books I've read

the inspiring courses I've had the
pleasure to attend

the mystical and powerful places
I've traveled to

the wonderful masters and teachers
I've met and learned so much from

the incredible students who attend my programs

the courageous clients who have been
open and ready to grow and share

the 'synchronicities' that have brought me
to this space now

the diverse and talented group of
friends and family that I have

... and all the amazing experiences that go
towards making up this delightful
adventure and dance called life!

Thank you!

YOU are more than
you think you are

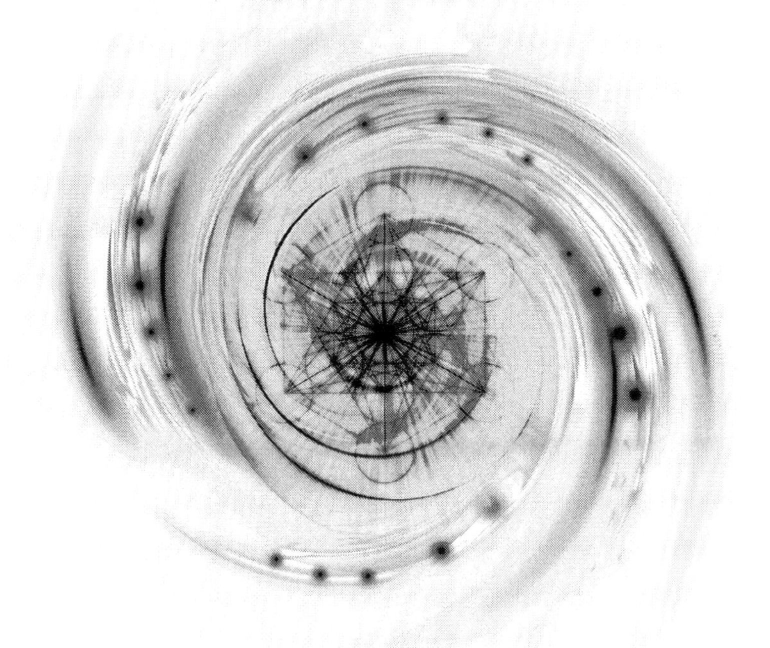

CAROL TALBOT

BOOK ONE

YOU the Divine Genius

YOU are more than you think you are

First published in 2016 by
Panoma Press Ltd
48 St Vincent Drive, St Albans, Herts, AL1 5SJ UK

info@panomapress.com
www.panomapress.com

Cover design by Michael Inns
Artwork by Karen Gladwell

ISBN 978-1-784520-97-7

A CIP catalogue record for this book is available from the British Library.

This book is available online and in all good bookstores.

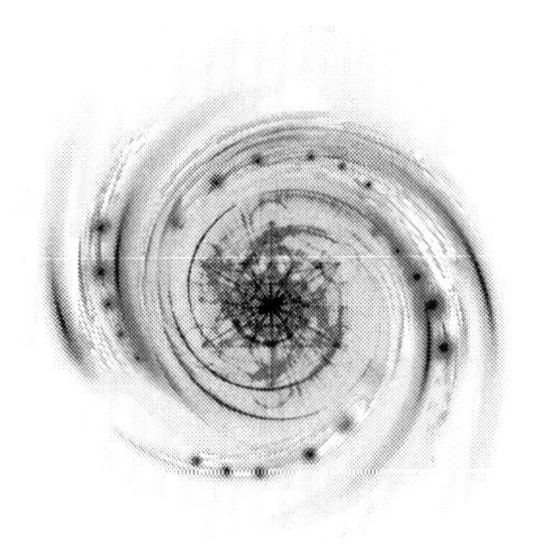

Contents

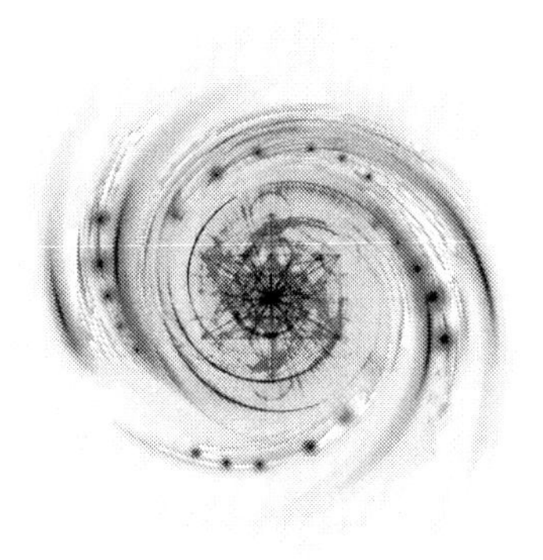

Acknowledgements

To be honest with you, writing another book was not on my 'have to, must do, should do, could do' list. In fact, in October 2015, during an Angel Reading with the talented and gifted Zoe Henderson, when I was told I would write another book, I just laughed and said I'd already done that and dismissed the comment.

Like the flicking of a switch from off to on, something changed within me early in January 2016 and I started exploring the possibility of putting this first book together to add order to thoughts and ideas that had been running around my head and heart for a few years. So my first thank you goes to Mindy Gibbins-Klein, for extraordinary sessions that helped me to 'give birth' and express what had lain dormant for some time.

Love, gratitude and appreciation to David Gross for the perfection of our connection. Thanks to you and 'we' for being so open in sharing gifts, insights and igniting an ever evolving conversation that leads us both in exciting directions.

The universe responded to my questions and desire for clarity in many different ways. One of those was in a stream of clients who were ready and willing to share their stories so you can also learn and grow from their experiences and challenges.

Numerous friends were ready to help, support and share experiences and insights including my amazing colleague and super-talented NLP Coach and Trainer, Wendy Shaw. I found more talent and support through Maggie Williams, Susan Furness, Julie-Ann Odell, Owen and Alexandra McKenzie, Jan Harrison, Paul Hendry, Sunil Jaiswal, Nadine Chammas, Michelle Chedotal, Tamara Pitelen, Kim Page, Peggy Phoenix Dubro, Michelle Karen, Khaled Ghorab, Nishi Shetty… to name just a few.

I have been blessed with great parents who gave me the biggest gift of all in allowing me to choose my own path and explore. My mother has shone lights in many directions for me during my life and, while I may not have always been appreciative at the time, I certainly am now.

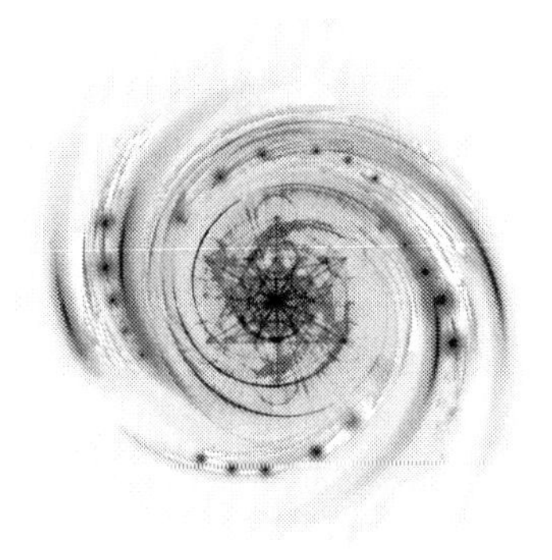

The Journey to your Divine Genius

- What am I really here to do?
- How can I contribute to the world in a meaningful way?
- Do I matter?
- How do I connect with a greater intelligence?
- How do I manifest my desires and get into vibrational alignment?
- How do I delete old habits and patterns and remove any blocks that are holding me back?
- How do I manifest a spiritual transformation?
- How do I attract and align with abundance?
- How do I love and accept who I truly am?
- How do I live a life beyond imagination?

If you are just a small part of a larger whole then how do you step into a fuller focus of who you are? How do you tap into all you really are to feel divinely guided and dance forward in life instead of stumbling and falling and tripping? How do you move with ease and grace from a 'seeing is believing' world to total trust in a 'believing is seeing' world where you can easily access the most resourceful parts of yourself or tap into the collective consciousness. Wouldn't it be useful to be able to access your very self from a different perspective?

If you drive a car, chances are that unless you're a mechanic (and you may well be), you don't know how every piece or part of the engine works. Yet you are still able to drive your car. But there's a big difference between driving a Ferrari and driving a Fiat. As you drive yourself and your body through life, once you understand all the components and parts that are available to support you and your journey, you'll have a deeper understanding of your abilities, potential and just how powerful you really are. After all, if you want to get good at any subject, you study that subject in depth. So the better you know yourself the better you are equipped to handle life's challenges and adventures.

It's time to create a new story. To be a better YOU!

This book is about YOU... and if you want to understand the huge extent of your capabilities and *who you really are*, then this first book in the series is an introduction to YOU and how you function in this space, time, dimension and reality. Here's a quick preview...

PART ONE - THE YOU-NIVERSE

Chapter One - You'll not only question the nature of reality, you'll understand how you experience YOUR reality. What really goes on in your head so that you see, hear and feel the world the way you do? Food for thought if you are ready to create a new and different reality.

Chapter Two - You have an extraordinary amount of choice in how you create your reality whether that is as simple as feeling good or bad, or the 'story' you have created for yourself and about yourself. The world around you is but a mirror of you and your inner world. So is what you're doing inside your head helping you or hindering you? You have the power to create a shift!

Chapter Three - If you've ever been in two minds, you're about to be introduced to both! Each of your two minds operates in a completely different way. When you discover how they are hard-wired to perform you'll understand how they can operate in harmony as well as how to tap into a deeper wisdom within.

Chapter Four - Whether you have a university degree or not, you are intelligence! In addition to discovering the power of the brain in your head, your heart and your gut, you'll find out that actually, every single cell in your body is intelligent. That's a huge intelligence network for you to discover and tap into.

PART TWO - UNLEARNING

Chapter Five - Are you beginning to notice the same patterns occurring and recurring in your life? Maybe it's certain people or situations that push 'hot buttons' that find you responding in a less than resourceful way. Through examining your thoughts and language you gain insights into your thought patterns and create new thoughts that expand your 'you-niverse.'

Chapter Six - It's your patterns in thinking and behavior that create your beliefs. Your beliefs shape your destiny so when was the last time you examined your beliefs and checked if they were up-to-date? Are your beliefs outdated and only supporting a limited view of what is really possible? It's time to choose your own beliefs rather than operate from those that have been passed down by your ancestors.

Chapter Seven - What is the 'story' that continues to shape your life? Are you ready to embrace a new identity? There is a liberation that can only come when you truly accept and love yourself for who you are. In some ways, that is a death of your old identity as you move towards acceptance and love.

PART THREE - EXPLORING

Chapter Eight - Just suppose you could 'stop the world!' If you want to discover and access different information then you need to know where to go and how to go effortlessly and easily into different states of being.

Chapter Nine - Do you believe in past lives? If you do, then it is quite possible that you arrived here for this lifetime with a purpose and plan. How can you access skills, talents or gifts from other lifetimes in the same way you would consult a library for additional information? Then there is the notion of life between lives to understand an even grander perspective.

Chapter Ten - The indigenous tribes of the world have lived, for the most part, in harmony with the earth, plants and animals. As they have deepened their connection to the earth there is much for you to learn from their traditions and understanding of the plants and animals.

PART FOUR - A NEW YOU-NIVERSE

Chapter Eleven - Everything is made up of shapes including you. What do the shapes in Sacred Geometry have to teach you about expanding consciousness and awareness and why are they relevant? Stretch your imagination and shape your life into a new direction.

Chapter Twelve - What has sound got to do with raising your frequency and vibration? When you hear sound you are hearing energy and when you create sound, you are creating energy. You'll discover that you and everything around you is energy vibrating at a specific frequency and vibration and that sound holds an important key to understanding your life.

Chapter Thirteen - It's time to fall in love with yourself for you are truly more than you think you are. When you change, everyone and everything else shifts too. It takes courage to move through the chaos; to make the commitment to be more than you think you are. When you do, you will discover that the possibilities are endless.

My wish is that this book will allow you to create opportunities to ignite and engage in the evolution of a different perspective for yourself and those around you; to step into a fuller focus of who you are!

On the road of life, there is always more to learn and discover! Our true purpose, in order to feel purpose-full, is to simply evolve and expand our wakefulness, awareness and consciousness!

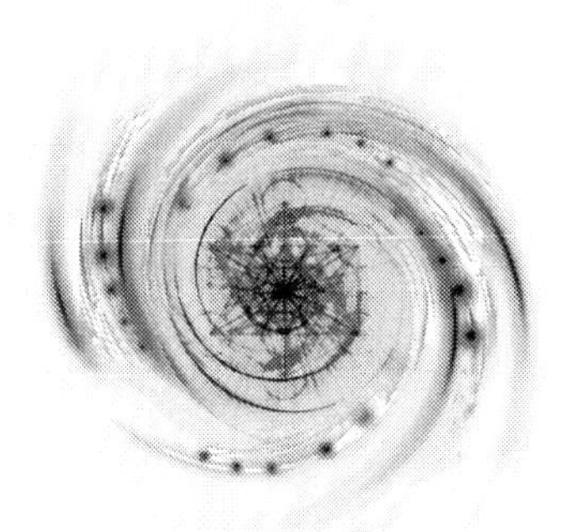

Part One:

THE YOU-NIVERSE

"It's the grace of your own existence
which drives all of creation"

Carol Talbot

I was totally alone in the middle of the world.

The Amazon rainforest spreads across 6.9 million square kilometers covering much of northwestern Brazil and extending into Colombia, Peru and other South American countries. Truly a wonder to behold! It is the world's largest tropical rainforest, famed for its immense biodiversity and crisscrossed with thousands of rivers.

An estimated fifty tribes native to the Amazon rainforest have a completely different perspective of the world, for many have never had any contact with the rest of the world. One tribe that has reached out to western civilization is the Achuar.

The Achuar live in a pristine area of the Ecuador rainforest without roads and far from the hustle and bustle and poverty present in many of our cities today. Instead, their life is filled with the richness of nature and the breathtaking beauty of their surroundings.

The energies of the indigenous tribes have always been focused on the land. Not just a land that offers to them water or food, I mean the actual energy of the dirt of the earth. Gaia is the energy they connect with (what we call Mother Earth and is also referred to as

'Pachamama') and in ancient times it was aligned with humanity in a society that is not nearly as complex as our society is now. Indigenous tribes experience the energies of being in partnership with the planet and with their ancestors who have gone before.

Flights to Kapawi Eco Lodge in Ecuador leave twice weekly from Shell, weather permitting. A small group of us took a flight from the small runway and within moments I experienced my first view into the heart and lungs of the world. My eyes immediately filled with tears and the experience touched my soul in an unexpected way. What a stunning world we inhabit. And how unaware most people are of the destruction many of life's daily actions cause to this important, and largely hidden part of the world.

Landing on a little strip of cleared rainforest and disembarking from the small aircraft, we were greeted by our Achuar guides who led us off the landing strip, down a narrow pathway to a group of boats waiting to take us to the award winning Kapawi Lodge, now managed and run by the Achuar tribes people themselves.

From the complexity of life in a city such as Dubai, where I live, to the pure simplicity of life in the rainforest, we slowly made our way along the Pastaza River. I wondered if David Attenborough was about to step out through the lush foliage which lined either side of the river, and we would discover we were in the middle of a BBC documentary!

Peaceful, clean, natural and inspiring, the rush and busyness of everyday life simply fades away. I felt that sense of excitement that sometimes accompanies the thrill of the unknown and a hint that something important was brewing. The excitement that builds when you begin the journey deep into the heart of YOU!

Let the journey begin...

Chapter One:

Your YOU-niverse

"Your experience of the outer world only becomes profound when you discover the connection it has to your inner world."

Carol Talbot

KEY QUESTIONS:

Why do you experience the world the way you do?

Why do others experience the world so differently?

What is reality?

How do you create YOUR reality?

Guess what? You cannot ever experience reality! That's a bold statement so let me first define 'reality.'

According to the Merriam-Webster Dictionary, reality is *"the state or quality of having existence or substance."*

So there you are, lying on soft, white sand on a beautiful beach that stretches for miles and miles, the vision of a clear blue sky above you and the sound of waves gently breaking on the shore close to your feet. Is this real or just a dream?

You're holding your breath as bright orange coals glisten in the dark just a few inches from your feet as you prepare to walk across burning hot coals of 1700 degrees Fahrenheit. Are the coals real? Is it really possible to walk across hot coals completely unharmed? Or is it all just an illusion?

You've built a business and risen to be well respected in your field of expertise. Despite all the acclaim and success you still feel something is missing. The passion you once had is no longer there and you wonder if it's time to let go. And then what? How do you move forward, and what do you move forward into so you can rediscover your passion? Does a new opportunity exist?

You know you're not happy in your relationship and the grass looks a lot greener on the other side. How do you let go without hurting anyone else and what if the grass turns out not to be so green? Did you really create this dilemma that seems so real?

Having worked for a respectable organization for over ten years, the company loses sight of their value of integrity. Out of the blue, and completely unexpectedly, you lose your job and on top of that, a bad financial investment means the future no longer looks bright. Is it real?

Or is everything in the whole universe that is not your problem the real reality?

In the classic movie, *The Wizard of Oz*, Dorothy and her dog Toto find themselves transported over the rainbow to the Land of Oz where they quickly discover that they have angered the Wicked Witch of the West. Their only hope of getting back to Kansas is to seek the help of the Wizard of Oz and so off they skip down the Yellow Brick Road towards the Emerald City.

On her journey, Dorothy is joined by a scarecrow that can't make up his mind because he doesn't have a brain. In fact, he believes himself to be a failure because he can't even scare a crow. They next encounter and rescue a tin man whose chest is empty and he desperately seeks a heart. Finally they meet a lion in desperate need of courage. All of them, the Scarecrow, Lion, Tin Man and Dorothy, believe that the Wizard of Oz has the power to grant their wishes.

Finally, they reach the Emerald City and after much pleading they are granted an audience with the great Wizard of Oz. He agrees to grant their wishes but only if they can perform one task – to bring him the broomstick of the Wicked Witch of the West.

Accepting the challenge they set off in search of the Wicked Witch of the West. Dorothy is captured but it is the Scarecrow, Tin Man and the Lion that secure her rescue and release. With the broomstick in their hands they return to the Wizard of Oz in order for him to fulfil his promise: brains for the Scarecrow, a heart for the Tin Man, courage for the Lion and the way home for Dorothy.

You too may be facing challenges in your life and may be joined, like Dorothy, by others along your journey. The Wizard of Oz demonstrated the power to provoke belief in Dorothy, the Scarecrow, the Tin Man and the Lion. All of them had demonstrated brains, heart and courage but it was the wizard who had the power to engender that belief in them. He awarded the Scarecrow a THD – Doctor of Thinkology, the Lion received a medal for his courage and the Tin Man a heart shaped clock for good deeds done. As for Dorothy, she realized that she had the power to help herself and had that power all along. It's a wonderful, heart-warming story which concludes with Dorothy waking up to find that the Emerald City, the Wizard of Oz and all the other characters were not real. It was all just a dream.

You too have all the power you need to help yourself on your journey. All the brains, heart and courage lie within you to create a magnificent reality.

The image below is a simplified visual representation of what is really going on inside your head and how what you choose to do inside your head impacts your reality. What you will discover is the huge amount of choice you actually have in what you can create.

How you create your reality

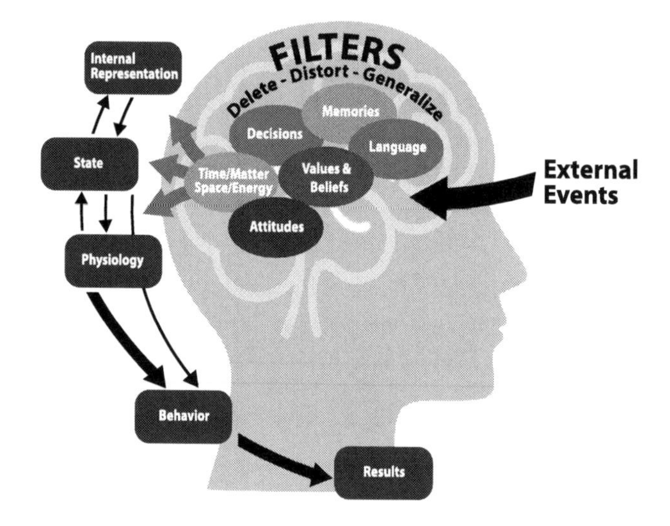

Your Universe

According to Hungarian psychologist, Mihaly Csikszentmihaly, people receive two million bits of information every single second of the day, streaming in to the nervous system through the eyes and ears and through the senses of touch, smell and taste. Your senses take in whatever you experience that you think is outside of you. But that is not all that is going on.

Actually you can only see a small bandwidth with your eyes and more exists. Your ears are only tuned to take in certain frequencies, which means that your eyes and ears are already limiting your perception of the world.

Whether it's a bead of sweat trickling down your back, a cool breeze raising the hairs on your arm, hearing your cat meowing or the bark of the dog next door, these stimuli enter through your senses and they are converted into neurological data. It's like light coming into a digital camera and being converted into digital data that can be stored and re-accessed later. Or taking a photograph and looking at the photograph later. So what you experience in your mind is not the world itself, but a neurological re-presentation of it. And your memories, images, impressions and all your thoughts, are all made up of patterns, shapes, arrangements and rearrangements of this neurological data.

If you think you have a busy mind, then just imagine two billion bits of information! Obviously if you were aware of all the information flooding into you through your five senses you would not be reading this book. You would go crazy! So what your mind does for you is it sifts the information through a set of filters (shown in the middle of the image) so you only become aware of the important 'stuff' to pay attention to. There are three main ways of filtering and sifting through all the bits of information bombarding you every second of the day.

The filters

First, your mind *deletes* information from your conscious awareness. Perhaps you have not noticed how the chair you're sitting on feels under your hips right now? Is the chair comfortable and soft, or hard? What about your feet, are they bare or are you wearing socks or shoes. How do they feel right now? Before I mentioned the chair and your feet, your mind was deleting that information because it probably wasn't important for you at this moment in time. In fact, you usually only become aware of the shoes on your feet if they are uncomfortable (like my super high heels!).

Perhaps you work in a noisy environment; I'm sure you're able to delete all the noise around you in order to hear what someone is saying on the other end of the telephone, or to focus on an important project.

I suspect you've also had situations where you've said something to someone and they acted as if they'd never heard it. "Joel, clean up your room." Sudden deafness! "You never said that to me," they protest and you know you did. For whatever reason, their mind has deleted the information from their conscious awareness.

Or perhaps you can recall a time when you thought you had lost your house or car key; you searched for it everywhere, that is until your friend brought the key back into your visual awareness! You had temporarily and visually deleted the information. Without deletion you would be faced with too much information to handle consciously. With deletion you can stay sane!

Then there's *distortion.* This is where you take the information that's coming in to you from the outside and make it into something that it's not. For example, you've probably had a situation where you've said something to someone and they've interpreted it in a completely different way. You may even have complimented a friend and they heard it as an insult. What they've done is distorted the information coming in and made it into something it wasn't.

Or you may have had an experience late in the night, waking up and being convinced someone had broken into your house only to discover it was the sound of the central heating system cooling down or the air conditioning. It makes that noise every night, but for some reason this time you thought it was an intruder. And even after you realized what it was, your heart was still pounding and you still had to check all the doors and windows! That's distortion.

Do you remember the song *Hotel California* by The Eagles? For years I thought the second verse said, "Her mind is definitely twisted, she's got the Mercedes Benz, she's got lots of pretty, pretty boys, that she calls friends." I was shocked when I saw the actual lyrics on a karaoke machine which are, "her mind is Tiffany-twisted." That didn't make any sense to me, so what I had done was distort the lyrics to the nearest sounding word that did make sense to me.

Distortion is actually the basis for many acts of creativity, planning and constructing imaginary futures. Using this filter you can create and enjoy works of art, music and literature. It also makes possible your ability to dream, envision, fantasize and plan for the future.

Next is *generalization*. This is where you take information and simplify it by saying it's the same as something else. Generalizations are actually very useful. If it weren't for generalizations you wouldn't be able to learn. For instance, you have generalizations for how a door works. When you approach a stranger's door for the first time, you don't have to figure out how it works. You know how door handles and hinges work in general and you simply look for the handle, lever or door knob and pull or push.

So generalizations are by and large useful, but not always, because they are not true in every case. In one experiment, researchers created a door with the handle on the same side as the hinges. People would struggle for ages trying to open it until they eventually gave up. Only a very small number would stop, think about it, and try pushing the other side of the door.

The process of generalization provides part of the explanation of how you are able to learn as rapidly as you do. If you drive a car then you have noticed that most cars are built in a similar way with the gears, steering wheel, brake, clutch and accelerator working in much the same way and often in the same place. That means once you've learned to drive one car; you can drive any car rather than having to relearn how to drive a car all over again when you buy a new car or rent one while you're on vacation. Generalization eliminates the necessity to relearn a concept or behavior every time you are confronted with a variation of the original.

Many supposedly new behaviors are actually composed of bits and pieces of previously experienced behaviors which are similar to the new behavior. Because of the similarity, you are able to generalize from the experience of the old behavior which means you do not need to learn the new behavior from the start. This saves a huge amount of time and energy in learning new behaviors.

So how do you create your specific filters so that you see, hear, feel and experience the world in the way that you do?

Your filters are made up of your ideas around time, space, matter and energy, your memories and the decisions you've made in your life as well as the things that are most important to you and your beliefs. Even your language is a filter and not just a means of communication. The world is made up of language and description. Language determines how you structure the reality that you create in your mind.

Let's do a little experiment here. Wherever you are right now, just take a look around at your surroundings, and while you are doing so, keep repeating silently to yourself the word brown, brown, brown. Keep repeating the word 'brown' for at least 30 seconds.

Now, close your eyes, and try to remember everything around you that is red. Not many things, are there?

Now, keeping your eyes closed, repeat to yourself the word red, red, red. Keep repeating the word 'red' for about 30 seconds. Now, open your eyes and look around. Notice how much redder your surroundings appear? You may even notice that as soon as you open your eyes they are immediately drawn to something that is red.

What you just did was change the language you were using, and it changed your perceptions of your surroundings.

Your memories and life experiences impact your filters and how you experience your world. It is your memories that impact how you choose to perceive yourself and the world around you. Your memories are stored in the brain and over time they have more and more impact over you and your world. You code your experiences differently according to whether an event or situation occurred in the past, if it is happening now or if it will happen in the future.

Just for a moment, bring to mind something that happened one week ago or one month ago and notice the direction that memory comes from (perhaps from behind you, or from the left). Now bring to mind something that will happen next week or next month, and again, notice the direction from which that future memory comes (often from in front of you or from the right). This should give you an indication that memories are coded differently so that you know the difference between something that is happening now, and something that happened in the past or something that will be happening in the future.

Your values also play a part in filtering information and bringing into your awareness what is important to you. Values do two key things for you. They give you upfront motivation such as getting up to go to work each day, and they also give you after the fact evaluation. So perhaps you review your day and evaluate whether you did a good job or not, or judge whether someone else did a good job or not. So if you take action, you take action because that particular action satisfies one of your values. After you have taken the action and you evaluate what you have done, how you know whether what you did was right, wrong, good or bad or just or unjust is because of your values. So they provide you with the motivation in the first place and then your measurement as far as whether that action was correct or incorrect, good or bad, right or wrong.

Behavioral psychologist, Morris Massey (and author of *The People Puzzle*) suggests that we go through a series of developmental periods that form and create our core values and what is important to us. The first is the imprint period which he suggests is from birth to around age seven. During the imprint period human beings are like walking sponges. You are literally soaking up *everything* that goes on around you, absorbing the beliefs and values of your parents, culture, religion and environment. You absorb and accept much of the beliefs and values of those closest to you without analyzing or judging. You may remember mimicking some of your parents' habits. I know I did... and got told off for it!

If you then compare and contrast values to beliefs, then beliefs are those convictions that we hold as being true and trust as being true. A belief is a thought that is thought so often that it creates physical, tangible results, which then reinforces the original belief. And your beliefs form the rules that you run your life on. They literally act as an on-off switch and are the driving force, like values, behind all your behavior, whether you know it or not. Dr. Bruce Lipton in his book *The Biology of a Belief*, says that your mind is designed to take your beliefs and turn them into reality. For example, if deep down you believe that you're not good enough, then you'll never have great friends because deep down, you do not believe you are good enough. You cannot have a great job or a great relationship because, deep down, you're not good enough. Unfortunately, human beings are driven to prove themselves right so 'believing that you're not good enough' becomes a self-fulfilling prophecy.

Your beliefs and values are both filters and both are secretly working in the background to either help you or hinder you.

Your attitude is really a collection of beliefs and values around a particular subject, while the decisions you have made and continue making are conclusions or resolutions reached after consideration or a choice you make. Of course your choices are colored by your previous experiences and impacted by your values, beliefs and attitude.

All of these, including your perception of time, space, matter and energy, impact your filters and how you experience the world and create your reality. Just for a moment consider other people around you and notice that what is important to them is often different from what you believe to be important. It could be as simple as being on time for an appointment. For some people that is really important and for others it is not. They have had different life experiences so they have different memories which mean they are running different filters. Think of your filters like wearing a tinted colored lens on a pair of glasses. It means the way you see, hear, feel and experience the world is different from the way others see, hear, feel and experience the world. No wonder it's often challenging to get on with other people!

Your filters also act like a magnet attracting you to certain situations, people and events and repelling you from others. Could it be that there is a pull and push acting as an unknown force in your life?

Like a magnet that sticks to certain metals, what is it that makes you drawn into certain situations? Why are you not drawn to other types of situations?

What you have been taught holds energy over you. In fact, your filters can keep you from seeing the whole picture. Perhaps you are operating from filters of doom and gloom or perhaps you are operating from the filters of possibilities.

Your filters create your interpretation of the world and likewise how you choose to interact and interpret the world's interaction with you. Think of it like a projection of light from a projector. Whatever color of light is projected on the screen alters the image on the screen.

It's like being given a pair of glasses at birth that colors how you experience the world. You might consider changing the glasses you are currently wearing and swap them for a newer, updated and technologically advanced pair!

So to do a quick review of your reality, you take in information from the outside world through your five senses and then run all the information through a set of filters – deletion, distortion and generalization – and your filters are made up from your memories, life experiences, values, beliefs, attitude, decisions, language as well as time, space, matter and energy. The remainder becomes your thoughts, or how you internally re-present information to yourself.

You think and internally re-present information to yourself in six ways at any given time: you see pictures and images, you hear sounds, and have feelings, tastes, smells and of course, you talk to yourself inside your head. Thankfully, it's perfectly acceptable to acknowledge that you talk to yourself now without being chastised as a little weird! Basically, you build your thoughts on the filtered information and it is through these thoughts that you perceive your world.

It's impossible to know what reality is. It is our senses, filters, beliefs and past experiences that give us a 'map of the world' from which we operate.

The Hindu culture has a word for this divide between our internal thoughts and the physical world, which they call 'maya,' meaning illusion. There's a wonderful allegorical story about six blind men coming across an elephant. The first one touches its trunk and says it is like a palm tree. Another touches its side and says it is like a rough wall. Another feels the elephant's tail and says it is like a piece of rope. Another touches its tusk and says it is like a spear. Another touches its leg and says it is like a tree. So each one of them has a different experience and each is convinced that their own explanation is the correct one and that the others are all wrong.

You cannot actually experience anything that is outside of your nervous system. So your internal representation is the reality in which you live.

It is not really what is going on outside. You cannot experience anything without it first being filtered by your nervous system.

So what does this tell you? That the 'maps' you are operating from - your thoughts - are not the actual territory, which is the physical universe outside of you. A map is a visual description of an area, but it is not the actual area. Or think of it like going to a restaurant and you're given a menu to choose what you want to eat. The menu describes the food, but it is not the actual food... unless it's an edible menu! Once you know this you are now stepping into your own power because you can change the map... you can change the menu! It enables you to change how you see and experience the world and have more choice. And as the physical world is an illusion, and all you really know about it is your thoughts of it, then you can change your thoughts, thereby changing your reality. Wow, how useful is that?

Your thoughts and feelings respond to what you are doing inside. This is the 'map but not the territory.' And this is how you can account for how people are so different. You may get ten different accounts of a party that ten people went to. Each one will have experienced the party differently. If you've ever been in an accident and hear the eye witness accounts from others who saw the accident occur, they will all give you a different explanation despite the fact that they all saw the same event. Or did they?

Here is something else for you to consider: if I'm working with a client, I may not know if they are making up their problem or not... and it doesn't matter! For example anxiety is an emotion of the future which means whatever they're anxious about has not happened, yet the thoughts that produce anxiety create very real feelings. Ask anyone who is about to do an important presentation for the first time!

"What is real? How do you define real? If you're talking about what you can feel, what you can smell, what you can taste and see, then 'real' is simply electrical signals interpreted by the brain." Morpheus from the Matrix

Let's plan your escape to a world that is open and allowing so you can be magnetized towards better situations, people and events.

Chapter Two:

Your Choice

"The world outside of you is simply a mirror."

Carol Talbot

KEY QUESTIONS:

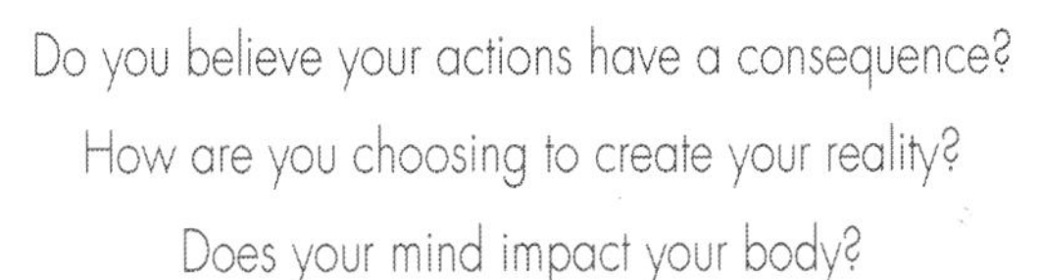

Do you believe your actions have a consequence?

How are you choosing to create your reality?

Does your mind impact your body?

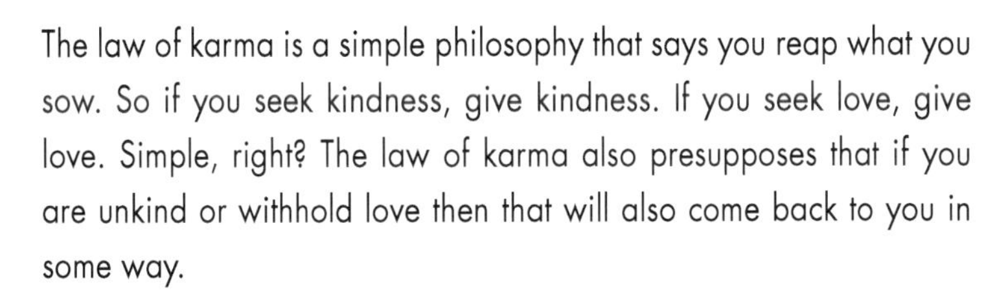

The law of karma is a simple philosophy that says you reap what you sow. So if you seek kindness, give kindness. If you seek love, give love. Simple, right? The law of karma also presupposes that if you are unkind or withhold love then that will also come back to you in some way.

In the Hindu and Buddhist traditions, karma is the sum of a person's actions in this and previous states of existence and viewed as deciding your fate in future existences. Karma can also be viewed as good or bad luck from your actions. Like throwing a pebble into a pond, your actions create a ripple effect in the universe which means that how you choose to think, act and feel today is going to have an impact on tomorrow and the days following.

Let's suppose you overslept in the morning, rushed to get ready to be on time for your first meeting, stubbed your toe on the corner of a chest of drawers, wished you had washed your hair the night before (assuming you have hair) and realized the shirt you want to wear needs an iron. You get stuck behind 'the slowest driver ever' and you feel a sense of irritation bubbling up. Does the meeting go well? Probably not!

Or up early with a sense of excitement about the possibilities of the day, you meditate for fifteen minutes followed by a walk, or a short yoga session. Enjoying your breakfast, you prepare for your first meeting, put on the clothes you prepared the night before and leave early to anticipate any traffic, arriving on time for your meeting. Does the meeting go well? Probably!

Running the same patterns of thinking and behavior, and operating with the same emotions day in and day out, is going to have an impact on your tomorrows as well as everyone and everything around you.

I was invited to a Global Mentoring Walk initiative to celebrate and honor International Women's Day. I had registered a few weeks earlier as a mentor and was assigned a mentee when I arrived at the event. After brief introductions, over 70 women started walking with their respective mentors and mentees. It must have been more than 40 minutes later before I could get a word in and contribute anything to my mentee as she tucked into her life story, complete with drama, illness, sacrifice and loss.

'How did you create this?'

This is the question that I often use to interrupt a 'story,' and it usually stops people in their tracks. 'You mean I've created my life this way?' Err, yes! Most people do not want to acknowledge responsibility for their life, their story and what is not working in their life. And for as long as they hold on to their story, it will continue to create a ripple effect across all areas of their life.

What's your story?

- I'm stuck in a job and situation that I don't like. Ask yourself, 'how did I create that?'
- My partner is never home and I feel unloved. Ask yourself, 'how do I choose to feel unloved?'
- I'm going through a major life crisis. Ask yourself, 'how am I creating this crisis?'
- I was in an accident that has led to ongoing health challenges. Ask yourself, 'how did I create an accident and for what purpose?'

It's time to consider yourself to be a bus driver, driving your life in different directions. Sometimes you pick up well-behaved passengers and sometimes they are unruly. The passengers are your thoughts and feelings. At times they can be rude, shouting out things like 'you're a reckless driver,' 'you're lost and have no idea where you're heading,' or 'get a move on!' They can be noisy too. If you are ready to grab the steering wheel and take your foot off the brake, then it is possible to change your story, reclaim your personal power and create a different ripple effect into your world.

Being the Cause for all the Effects in your life!

First, you need to decide to be the Cause for all the Effects in your life because, like it or not, Cause and Effect appears to be a rule of how the universe works. Isaac Newton told us so. There was Newton, sitting under an apple tree, and an apple fell on his head. Why? Because of gravity. It didn't just happen haphazardly or because the apple wanted to fall on his head.

And life's like that.

If Newton had simply rubbed his head and thought, 'bother, why are these things always happening to me?' he'd have been on the Effect side of the equation. Newton chose how to interpret the apple falling on his head. For most people it would have been an Effect. For him it became a Cause, and the Effect this has had on the educated world since then has been astounding.

The important thing is whether you choose to think of yourself as being on the Cause side of the equation or on the Effect side.

This is a very useful way of thinking about the *physical* world because, once you understand what causes things to happen, you can start to control what happens. For instance, one morning your car won't start. The battery is flat. And that is what is causing the car not to start. So you recharge or replace your battery and lo and behold, it starts. Great.

Life and existence is a chain reaction of Causes and Effects. Everything that happens was caused by what happened before, and is the effect for what will happen next. And the beauty about being a human is, you have a brain, you have consciousness, you have free will, and you can choose how to respond to any given circumstances. You have an infinite possibility of choices. Anything from cursing your bad luck for being hit by a falling apple to writing a brilliant scientific paper. When you choose to curse your bad luck, you're at Effect. When you choose to write a paper, you're at Cause.

So what does all this mean for you? It means there are some people who habitually think of themselves on the Effect side of life, bemoaning their bad luck that apples are always falling on their head. They're the ones who say, 'I have a problem.'

Sonya is a highly intelligent woman in many ways, yet continually fails to grasp her own personal power. Her 'story' is sad with a history of abusive relationships, a financial investment failure and working for a company that has let go of a lot of staff which gives her a constant feeling of insecurity. Granted, she is proactive in her own personal development, attending programs, seminars and personal healing sessions. Yet, as long as she leaves her healing and fate to others, she will continue to run the same patterns and feel powerless, on the 'Effect' side of the equation, rather than power-full and on the 'Cause' side of life.

Here are some examples of what people say when they are at 'Effect.' 'I didn't achieve my goal of being fit and healthy because being overweight runs in our family, it's genetic.' 'I didn't get the job I wanted because I don't have a degree.' 'My poor health holds me back.' 'I don't have enough money to do anything to change my situation.' 'I have responsibilities.' 'I can't change.'

There are other people who habitually think of themselves on the 'Cause' side of life, always doing and achieving things. They're the ones who, rather than have problems, say 'I have a challenge.'

What do you think it is that determines whether they are at Cause or Effect? Could it be anything to do with what is going on in their head and how they choose to perceive the outside world?

These are the sort of things people say when they are at Cause. 'I was determined to feel healthy so I got the whole family involved and we workout together every day.' 'I decided it was about time I had a degree so I've begun taking evening classes.'

If you know people like this, chances are they are happier, more optimistic and definitely more fun to be with.

I remember a particularly frustrating call with one of my mentors. He asked me (and you can give this a go too) to hold out each hand and imagine I was holding an ice cream cone in each hand. One cone had vanilla ice cream and the other had chocolate ice cream (pick the flavors you want). I then had to decide which one I wanted. When I picked the chocolate one he asked me 'why?' Sharing that I loved chocolate ice cream and it was my favorite, he simply said 'no, wrong answer,' and asked me again, which one I wanted. This scenario went on for some time before I finally said 'BECAUSE I CHOOSE CHOCOLATE!' Bingo!

So you are consciously and unconsciously creating your life as you go along by what you CHOOSE to pay attention to, how you CHOOSE to interpret what you experience, how you CHOOSE to feel about that interpretation and how you CHOOSE to act as a result.

Cause and Effect as a pathway to personal power has actually now been proven by quantum physics. Austrian scientist Erwin Schrödinger was instrumental in the development of quantum mechanics. He set up an imaginary experiment in which a closed box would contain a live cat and a tube of poison, arranged in a way that if radioactive decay occurred then the poison container would be broken and the cat would die. (Remember that this was an imaginary experiment and no cats were involved!) In the everyday world, there is a 50% chance that the cat will be killed and a 50% chance that the cat will not be killed. Without looking inside the container there is no way of knowing whether the cat is dead or alive.

So just suppose a friend of yours opens the box and the cat is dead... except your friend decides not to tell you. That means, in your world, the cat could still be dead or alive. This is the Observer Effect in action and not only that the observer brings the observed into being, but also that nothing in the universe exists as an actual 'thing' independently of our perception of it. Schrödinger's experiment implies that observation – the very involvement of consciousness, gets the cement to set. It implies that reality is not fixed, but fluid and mutable, and hence open to influence!

Cause and Effect is the Observer Effect and how you create the effects in your universe. You are continually observing your universe into being. And remember, you cannot prove anything outside of yourself and you experience your universe through your senses, the nervous systems and the filters you have created.

Once you realize that you are creating your life as you go along, it gives you the power to change. You can choose to pay attention to different things; choose to interpret your experiences differently; you can choose to feel differently; and you can choose how to act differently.

Results versus excuses

It sounds simple and easy enough, yet let's face it, like many people, you probably enjoy a good moan, groan, grumble and complain. Well, it appears in life that you always get one of two things: either you get the results you want, or you get reasons or excuses for not getting the results you want.

Let's say you order outside catering for a special occasion to be delivered at 6pm, giving you time to set everything up before the first guests arrive. The company confirms the order and delivery time.

The delivery time comes and goes and still no catering has arrived. "Sorry we were rushed off our feet, we ran out of a couple of items and some of our staff were late." All the reasons and excuses you can imagine for not having done what they had agreed to do.

So in life you either get what you want, or you get reasons and excuses for not getting what you want.

Just for a moment imagine a time in the future when you didn't have any reasons and all your excuses had disappeared. What you would be left with is results!

I believe the person who is massively successful doesn't believe their reasons and doesn't buy into their excuses. They know they'd be lying to themselves. So they get rid of them. They make sure they've got enough flour; they make sure the motorcycle is serviced; they make sure the staff are trained properly; they even introduce backup systems and contingency plans. They won't accept any reasons or excuses, so the only possible outcome left is success!

Of course the choice is yours. You can be successful or you can believe your reasons and excuses.

The mirror effect

It was psychologist Carl Gustav Jung who proposed that whatever you perceive outside of yourself, in people, in events, in situations, in circumstances, are all actually projections from inside of you, like a reflection in a mirror.

What this means is, it is never the external person, event, situation or circumstance that's the problem. It is actually a problem within yourself that you are projecting onto a person, event, situation or circumstance outside of yourself.

The late Steven Covey said, "We do not see the world as the world is. We see the world as we are."

Jessica was annoyed by her sister Jill's behavior. It really bothered her. "I've given her a job, bought her a car and helped her numerous times in the past. Not once has she shown any gratitude or said 'thank you'!" Jill has a belief that she deserves to be bought things and be taken care of. If the outside world is a mirror and reflection of our inner world, then what bothers us about others is what we have suppressed or rejected in ourselves. So Jessica discovered that she had a belief that she was not worthy of being bought things or taken care of and her outside world reflected that belief through her sister.

The world outside of you is a mirror!

There is an old Chinese Taoist story of a farmer in a poor country village. He was considered wealthy because he owned a horse which he used for transportation and ploughing. One day the horse ran away. All his neighbors said how terrible it was, but the farmer simply said, "Maybe!" A few days later the horse returned and brought two wild horses with it. The neighbors were amazed at his good fortune, but the farmer just said, "Maybe." The next day the farmer's son tried to ride one of the wild horses and fell off, breaking his leg. The neighbors offered their sympathy for his misfortune, but the farmer just said, "Maybe." The next week conscription officers came to the village to take young men for the army. They rejected the farmer's son because of his broken leg. The neighbors said he was lucky, but once again, the farmer said, "Maybe."

Everything that you perceive outside of you is a projection from your thoughts, from inside of you and at the unconscious level; your perceptions of events, your perceptions of people, your perceptions of people's motivations are projected from inside of yourself, mostly at the unconscious level. Actually, when you describe another person, it often says more about you than the other person!

Rajesh complained that his father was arrogant and disrespectful and this was the reason for not allowing his son to meet his grandfather. The 'mirror effect' allowed Rajesh to realize that he, himself, was being arrogant and disrespectful too, by blocking his son's wish to build a relationship with his grandfather.

Carl Prebum and David Bohm postulated that the universe is a hologram. The question then being 'what is it a hologram of?'

First, a hologram is a 3-dimensional photograph manufactured with the aid of a laser. In addition to being 3-dimensional, the image recorded differs from a conventional photograph in a very important way. If you cut a normal photograph in half, each half contains half of the image from the original photograph. If you cut a hologram in half and shine a laser through one of the sections you will find that each half still contains the entire image of the original hologram. Each tiny section contains its own information and every other bit of information as well.

With holograms, you can recreate yourself. The difference between a hologram and what you perceive is real is density. After all, you can put your hand through a hologram!

Just for a moment consider a dream. It's real... until you realize it's a dream. Could it be that you're projecting a hologram while you sleep?

The universe is a hologram of 'YOU!' The universe is a waking dream of your projection and you are a living hologram.

This is insightful because when people say things that are a little bit odd, unusual, out of context, or in your opinion unrealistic, it is worth asking yourself, who are they really talking about? Are they talking about the person or situation they say they are talking about, or are they really talking about themselves? On the other hand there might be some things that you look at in the outside world and you go, wow, that's my projection, that's really good.

For example, during a personal development program, a student will be describing someone else's problem behavior, such as their mother, and everyone else who's listening will say, "That's not your mother you're describing, that's you!"

The good news is that this means the place to solve a problem is inside you. When people push the problem away from themselves onto other people, events, circumstances and situations, they are also pushing away the solutions. It's just another form of making excuses. So stop making excuses, stop projecting it outside yourself. Bring the problem back inside you, and there you can tackle it and change it.

You can change how you observe your world as well as the people and situations in it.

Your mind and body are connected

You probably learned in school that the mind controls the body through the central nervous system. It sends electrical impulses to muscles which causes them to contract or relax and that's how we move our limbs. There's also the autonomic nervous system which controls involuntary activities, such as your heartbeat and digestion, and the endocrine system that controls the chemical balances of the body.

But none of these explain the phenomena of mind over matter such as people who can slow their heartbeat down and even make it stop and start. Or people who can cure themselves of incurable illnesses simply through positive thinking. Or tribal people who can pierce themselves with skewers without bleeding. Medical science used to dismiss these things as rubbish because they couldn't find any mechanisms to explain them.

It wasn't until the late 1960s that neurotransmitters were discovered. Neurotransmitters are chemicals that travel through the body carrying messages. Since the 1990s this led to a whole new field of study which is called neuropsychopharmacology (get your tongue around that name!). Neuropsycholpharmacology is a science that involves the possible effects of drugs on the brain and the behavior they may cause.

Deepak Chopra, in his book, *Quantum Healing,* described it by saying every single cell in your body is bathed in neurotransmitters. Every single cell in your body is eavesdropping on your internal dialogue. What this means to you is that every single cell in your body knows what you are thinking.

Here's a quick experiment so you can experience the mind body connection directly.

Stand up for a moment and put both arms straight out in front of you with the palms of your hands facing the floor and then close your eyes (so you'll need to read through these instructions first). Turn your right hand up towards the ceiling and imagine a big heavy book resting on your right hand. Better still, imagine a stack of books resting on your right hand. Notice how heavy they feel and you might even notice that if you hold them there for even 30 seconds, your right arm is beginning to get tired and moves downwards.

With your eyes still closed, imagine that tied to the back of your left hand is a huge bunch of helium balloons and notice that your left arm feels lighter and starts to lift up... while your right arm feels heavier and heavier with the weight of the books. Keep your arms where they are and open your eyes.

If there has been any change in the relationship between your left and right arms, take that as a sign that you are suggestible (maybe your right arm is now a lot lower than your left arm).

Now you know there never were any books resting on your right hand or balloons attached to your left wrist. The books and balloons were in your mind and your body followed the suggestions you gave it.

Consider the impact on the physical body of thoughts that you hold for a whole day, or a week, or a month, or a year, or five years, 10 years, 20 years. Could you then begin to understand why so many people develop psychosomatic illnesses and dis-eases in their body? Negative thoughts in the mind such as 'I'm not good enough,' 'I don't deserve anything better,' 'I'll never amount to anything,' and low self-esteem or negative emotions have a huge impact on your body.

Peter was desperate for a break. Heading up a chain of schools he was tired and badly wanted a break before the end of the term. Taking a hike during the weekend to enjoy the fresh air and clear his head, he slipped and fell. Guess what? He broke his leg and on doctor's orders was advised to take a 'break' from work and to rest. Careful what you wish for!

You have the power to change the way you think!

Responsibility for results

You are probably reading this because you want to learn more about yourself. Now I can guide you through the process of learning, but I can't learn for you. I am going to be giving you information and explanations and exercises but I can't remember for you, I can't reason for you, and I can't do the exercises for you. And when the book is complete I can't improve your relationships. I can't lose weight for you. I can't get you the promotion you want. I cannot change your life for you or create a spiritual transformation for you. Only you can do that, and you have the power.

So the responsibility for change lies completely, totally, one hundred percent within the person who wants and needs to make the change. Not with a coach, not with a therapist, not with a manager, not with a friend, not with a trainer, but with the person who needs and wants to make the change.

If a person doesn't want to change, there is absolutely nothing you can do. If you want to change somebody's mind and they don't want to change their mind it won't work because the responsibility for change lies totally with the person making the change.

You have the power to choose to be the Cause for all the Effects in your life and you've got to be willing to give up all of your excuses. If you are willing to take responsibility you will begin to see your life and the world as a gift.

Chapter Three:

Your Two Minds

"Of course it is happening inside your head, Harry, but why on earth should that mean that it is not real?"

Albus Dumbledore - J.K. Rowling's *Harry Potter and the Deathly Hallows*

KEY QUESTIONS:

What's the difference between the conscious mind and the unconscious mind?

Is it possible to consciously change a behavior?

Is there such a thing as a bad memory?

Should you turn left or should you turn right? Should you stay or will you go? If you've ever felt like you're in two minds, allow me to introduce you to your conscious mind and your unconscious mind.

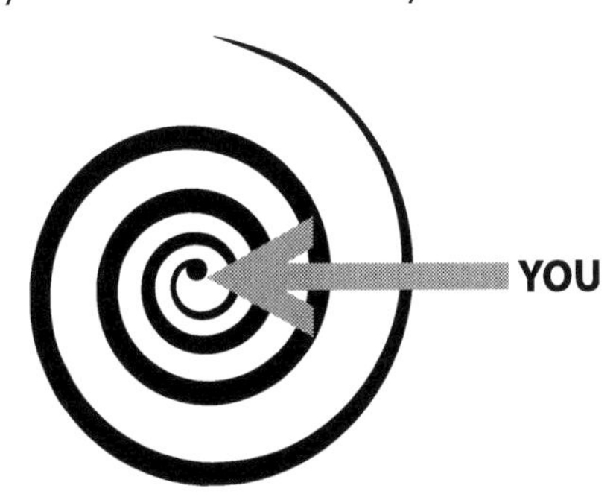

Imagine a spiral and where you are now is the point in the middle of the spiral. That is your conscious awareness and who you are now, who you believe yourself to be and where you are in your world of awareness. Your unconscious mind is that which is spiraling outwards as it absorbs and takes in *everything* around you through your five senses and in this chapter you're going to discover just how powerful it is in terms of shaping and driving your life.

The conscious mind is the part of your mind that is responsible for logic and reasoning and it is where you associate with who you are as a human being. Your conscious mind is constantly analyzing, criticizing and judging everything and everyone around you. For example, the other year I was presenting at a women's event and decided to start my presentation in a dressing gown and slippers. Well, the organizer had told me to wear something I felt comfortable in! The point I wanted to make was that most of the women would have been busy in their own heads criticizing and judging my dress sense or inappropriate attire because that is what the conscious mind does. It also acts a little like a gate keeper. So if someone is presenting you with information or ideas that are different from your own then your conscious mind is going to challenge that information or those ideas.

Your conscious mind is the mind that you think with. It is logical and rational using linear, sequential thinking and has a very narrow, laser-like focus. It can only process or focus on approximately seven, plus or minus two things at one time. The key here is the phrase, *at one time.* The conscious mind can only process about seven bits of information at a time, and it processes the information incredibly quickly.

You've probably heard the phrases, 'a stream of consciousness,' or 'a train of thought.' And that is exactly what it is. The person reciting poetry is only consciously aware of about the next seven words, and by the time they have quoted them, they have already moved on to the next seven words, and so on.

Consider this, when you write down your telephone number, you probably do it in clusters of about three or four digits. This is because you can only consciously think of a small number at any one time.

I'm sure you have had to fill in your 16 digit credit card number when making an online purchase. So how do you actually do it? Well, you probably look at the first cluster of four digits on your card, memorize them in your conscious mind, and then look at the computer monitor to type them in. Then you look at the next four numbers on the card, type them in and the next, and the next. And when you've finished, if someone covered your eyes and asked you what the first four digits were, you wouldn't know! Well not consciously. But you would be able to remember them if you had trained yourself in the art of remembering.

Your conscious mind gives instructions, whereas your unconscious mind follows instructions. So consider your conscious mind and unconscious mind like a rider and a horse. It's the rider of the horse that sets the direction, the goal and outcomes. After all, it wouldn't be very useful having a horse set your goals for you! It's the horse, the unconscious mind, which helps you reach your destination. So your conscious mind is the goal setter and the unconscious mind is the goal getter. And they need to work together in harmony so that the horse (your unconscious mind) knows where the rider (the conscious mind) is heading.

The times you are most fully conscious are when you are trying to solve a problem. Like a mathematician, or a scientist, or a mechanic trying to figure out why a car won't start. It's a very useful state to be in because your powers of logic and inductive and deductive reasoning are all in overdrive. And so are your critical faculties, and skepticism. But even scientists and mechanics aren't in this state all the time. As soon as they leave work, and drive home, they'll probably lapse into a light trance. And at the weekend, digging the garden, washing the car or walking the dog, they'll daydream just like everyone else with thoughts coming and going here and there, with no apparent reason behind them. This is often when you will be the most creative. Perhaps you know the story of the Greek philosopher and scientist Archimedes who had his 'eureka' moment sitting in the bath, or the scientist who unraveled the structure of DNA *dreamt* of the double helix. And dear old Einstein said, "Imagination is more important than knowledge. Knowledge is limited. Imagination circles the world."

Cognitive neuroscientists conclude that the conscious mind contributes only about 5% of our cognitive activity. That means that 95% of our decisions, actions, emotions, and behaviors are derived from the processing of the unconscious mind!

Imagine going into a huge, vast, darkened warehouse with a flash-light. What you can see is only what is lit up by your flashlight and what you are pointing it at. However, it doesn't mean that the rest of the warehouse does not exist. The light merely indicates what you are consciously shining your flashlight on and is within your awareness, such as your problem. Your unconscious mind is everything else! So how does it work?

The unconscious mind and how it works

Well, your unconscious mind works on intuitions, gut feelings and instincts which happen instantaneously, which is why your unconscious mind can be aware of two million things all at the same time. Information is registered at the unconscious mind level at least half a second before registering at the conscious level. This was discovered after years of research by neurologist Benjamin Libet who performed a sequence of remarkable experiments in the early 1980s. And it's important.

Just for a moment consider a time when perhaps you've been cut off in traffic and instantly got upset, angry and stressed for hours as you replayed the experience over and over again in your mind. Consciously, you make the decision that the next time that you get cut off in traffic you'll stay calm and just let it go. A good plan! However, next time you get cut off by another driver you find yourself instantly upset, angry and stressed again, even though you had consciously decided to respond differently. The challenge is that the information and experience of being cut off in traffic hits the unconscious mind first, thereby activating an automatic and conditioned response. What this means is that you need to get to know your unconscious mind if you really want to initiate permanent changes. In fact, all learning, all behavior and all change is the domain of your unconscious mind.

If I ask you to tell me your telephone number you can reel it off instantly, effortlessly and easily. But where was the information before I asked for it? That's right, safely stored away in your unconscious mind. Indeed, it is believed that everything you have ever learned in your entire life is stored in your unconscious mind. Everything!

The unconscious mind is an astonishingly powerful information processor that can record perceptual experiences and forever play them back at the push of a button. Interestingly, you often only become aware of your unconscious mind's push button programs when someone else 'pushes your buttons.' As one of my friends' mother often says, "I installed the programs and buttons when you were a child and I can push them." And she does!

What this means for you is if you want to bring about significant changes in yourself and your behavior, you have to do so at the unconscious level, as well as at the conscious level.

Theories about the unconscious mind vary widely within psychological circles. Sigmund Freud referred to the unconscious mind as where we hold all our dark, murky memories, desires and secrets. Cognitive psychology's view is that that the unconscious mind is simply a mixture of cognitive processes that we're not aware of. The field of NLP (neuro linguistic programming) holds the view that the unconscious mind is the seat of wisdom and advises working with it rather than against it.

Just how big is this unconscious hard drive of yours? Well just consider this; you began life as a single cell, so small it can't even be seen by the human eye. And a tiny part of this cell is the nucleus, and inside this are the 46 pairs of chromosomes that make you, 23 of which came from your mother and 23 from your father. And these chromosomes are made from strings of DNA, which have been described as the most extraordinary molecule on earth. And this microscopic DNA speck is the microcosm of you, the complete you in miniature. It determines your sex, your height, the color of your hair, the color of your eyes. It is a complete blueprint of every muscle, every bone, every organ and every single cell of your entire body. If you wanted to write down the number of possible combinations of data that your DNA contains and simply print the figure on paper, the number would be so long it would fill more than five thousand average size books, and that's a lot of zeros. That's the information that is stored in a minute dot which is inside another minute dot too small to be seen.

In the 1950s, neurosurgeon Wilder Penfield was the first person to bring to the media the idea of genes storing permanent records of the past, and that these memories are hidden away from the conscious mind, either by choice or blocked by trauma, fears, phobias etcetera. Thank goodness. I mean if all your memories with negative emotions attached to them were at the front of your mind, it would be challenging to get through the day without bursting into tears every few minutes, let alone carry out daily tasks. So your unconscious mind represses those memories until an appropriate time when it may bring that memory into your conscious awareness to deal with. Perhaps a certain song will jog your memory or a friend will use certain words or a tone of voice that brings up a memory. Rather than deal with any repressed memories with negative emotions most people push them back down to remain hidden, until they shout even louder, often through the manifestation of illness or disease. Then you are compelled to look deeper within for the root cause of the physical manifestation of unattended negative emotions.

Your unconscious mind runs your body and all your behavior. If you put your hand on a hotplate, do you think 'Gosh that's hot! It could hurt me. I'd better take my hand off. Now which muscles do I have to use to lift my hand up?' Not a bit of it! Your unconscious mind has snatched your hand away before your conscious mind has even had time to think about it. In fact, your unconscious mind runs every single function of your body whether you are awake or asleep.

Here's an experiment. Rest your hand on a table and drum your fingers rapidly, like someone who is bored and waiting for something to happen. Give it a go now.

Now, how did you do that? Did you think, 'right, first I'll raise my little finger, closely followed by my second finger, closely followed by my third finger, and then my forefinger, and just as my forefinger comes up, I'll drop my little finger down with a thump, closely followed by my second finger, closely followed by... etcetera, etcetera.'

It would be an amazing feat to drum your fingers by conscious willpower, and likely a slow process. It's your unconscious mind at work.

The point of this is that every single behavior that you demonstrate, good, bad or ugly, is actually run by your unconscious mind. So if you want to change a behavior, you cannot do it by willpower alone, you have to get into the unconscious mind and change it there. Similarly, if you want to run a new program on a computer, you have to install the program first or upgrade the existing software.

Here's another experiment and this time it is a thought experiment.

Imagine a plank of wood lying on the ground. Building planks are usually seven inches wide; that's about 18 centimeters, which is perfectly wide enough to walk on. Now mentally decide to walk along that plank. What actually happens? Your conscious mind sends an instruction to your unconscious mind to walk along the plank, and your unconscious mind does it. Simple. Easy. No problem.

Now, imagine the same experiment, the same plank of wood, only this time it is suspended on scaffolding 100 meters in the air, that's about the height of a 40 floor building. What happens this time? Your conscious mind sends an instruction to your unconscious mind to walk on the plank. The whole time your conscious mind keeps thinking, 'don't fall off the plank,' but your unconscious mind cannot process negatives. It simply cannot understand the word 'don't'. So all it is hearing is, FALL OFF THE PLANK, FALL OFF THE PLANK. And that's why most people aren't tightrope walkers.

It's also why diets invariably don't work. Because people on diets are constantly thinking, 'don't eat food,' whereas their unconscious mind is hearing 'EAT FOOD.'

Here's an example of an instruction that is given knowingly. Let's say a man has a heart-wrenching break-up and a really stressful divorce. He is feeling miserable, so he says to himself, "I never want to feel this bad again, so I'm never going to fall in love again." Years later he's in a fantastic new relationship and yet the one thing that is holding the relationship back is that he cannot allow himself to love. On a conscious level he may even have forgotten that he'd ever made that negative statement to himself. Possibly he thinks he is incapable of love, or that love is some nonsense out of romance novels and doesn't exist in real life. Really it is because he is following an instruction he gave his unconscious mind and that program is still running at the unconscious level. A new program and instruction needs to be installed and the old program deleted.

Your unconscious mind maintains all of your instincts and generates habits. This is your fight or flight response. You don't consciously choose to send adrenalin coursing around your bloodstream, it happens as a direct response to a sign of danger and it is hardwired into your nervous system. Your instincts are there to keep you safe, like snatching your hand away from that hotplate.

Habits are also things you do without thinking about them, but they are things you have learned to do, like driving a car. The first few times you did them you did them consciously, and as you repeated them over and over again they became a habit. You've probably heard the saying that it takes 21 days to make or break a new habit. And if you've visited the pyramids in Cairo, Egypt, you'll know that you can hire a horse to trek around the pyramids. It doesn't matter whether you've ever ridden a horse before or not, because the horse will take the same route it takes every day, and has done for years. If you fall off the horse, it will just keep going the way it has always gone and if you do want to go in a different direction you'll need to hold on to the reins tightly and continue to steer it in a new direction.

That time frame can be dramatically shortened with some of the techniques from the NLP (neuro linguistic programming) toolbox.

When I say 'dramatically,' I mean shifting an unwanted behavior in ten minutes or less!

Your unconscious mind continually wants to seek more and more. Let's say you've finally achieved a long sought after goal, the euphoria and celebration probably lasts a week, maybe a little longer. Before long, you want more. That is your unconscious mind continually spiraling you forward to expand your world and it means there will never be a time where there isn't anything to learn.

Your unconscious mind takes things literally! And this is why you have to be very precise when you ask your unconscious mind to do something for you, both in what you ask it to do, and when you want it done by. For example, if you want more money and your focus is more money, your unconscious mind will get to work on that straight away. Perhaps you'll see a coin on the street, pick it up and think nothing of it. Meanwhile, your unconscious mind is going 'Yippee! He asked for more money and I gave him more money. Job done!' You might want to be more specific next time!

Your conscious mind is creative and it requires an operating system, which is your unconscious mind. Your unconscious mind is a recording device taking in everything and then it acts as a playback device running your habits, instincts and behaviors that are your inbuilt programs. Your unconscious mind is something you want to connect with so that you can understand which programs, patterns and behaviors are working for you and what is working against you. This is when you can expand the horizon of what is possible. Your unconscious mind knows what you need to know about you because it has recorded everything for you. To enable you to be who you want to be, do what you want to do and to have what you want to have, it would be good to get to know it!

Chapter Four:

You are Intelligence!

"From a single cell you unravel and evolve
... all from a single cell!"

Carol Talbot

KEY QUESTIONS:

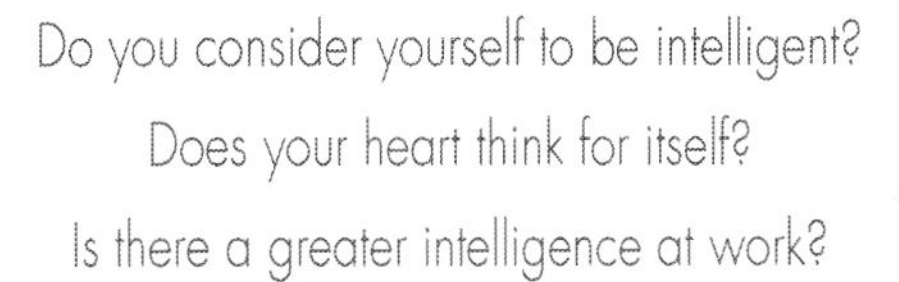

Do you consider yourself to be intelligent?

Does your heart think for itself?

Is there a greater intelligence at work?

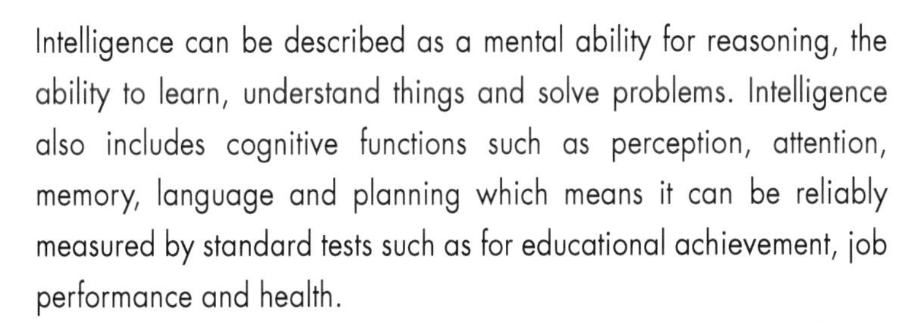

Intelligence can be described as a mental ability for reasoning, the ability to learn, understand things and solve problems. Intelligence also includes cognitive functions such as perception, attention, memory, language and planning which means it can be reliably measured by standard tests such as for educational achievement, job performance and health.

As you read this perhaps you're eating an apple. With your senses you can see it, taste it, hear the crunch as you bite into it and taste the sweetness and juiciness of it. Then it passes into your body and you forget about that mouthful as you take another bite of the apple. However, within you so much intelligence is required to orchestrate cells, digestive juices and organs functioning in a way that your body absorbs the nutrients that it requires from the apple and discards what is not needed.

- What intelligence is at work to know what you need from that bite of an apple?
- What intelligence decides what is kept and what is discarded?
- What intelligence informs the whole body what to do as it kicks into the act of digesting that piece of apple?
- Is it your heart that is noticing what it feels like to eat an apple or is it the brain telling your body what to do?

So let's talk about your brain

Your brain is a focusing mechanism and the average adult human brain weighs in at around 1.5kg and has a mushy texture (sorry, not a very technical term for the brain) and supposedly controls everything that you do and think. It is a remarkable organ that is built of nerve cells, or neurons to be precise, and about 100 billion of them. Every neuron has a connection at either end; a dendrite and the long axon. These two connect together to form the many pathways of the brain.

What is so incredible is the massive number of neurological connections going on between these cells. The estimate is 100 billion neurons constantly wiring and firing together. The phrase 'neurons that wire together, fire together,' can be attributed to neuropsychologist, Donald Hebb, and really means that each experience you encounter, including your feelings, thoughts, sensations, and muscle actions become embedded in the network of brain cells that produce that experience. Each time you repeat a particular thought or action, you strengthen the connection between a set of brain cells or neurons. The most obvious example of this would be driving a car to the point where you no longer step into your car and think 'how do I start the car and drive?' You do it automatically. Literally, your patterns of behavior and response become hard wired!

Your brain is divided into different parts. There are the outer layers which make up the cortex which is divided into left and right hemispheres. The right controls the left side of the body and the left controls the right side of the body.

Different areas of the cortex are responsible for different functions, for example, visual processing takes place at the back of the skull, while the side on the left hemisphere is concerned with speech and language. Sensory areas and motor systems fill the next area, with the frontal lobes responsible for complex planning, behavior and social awareness. Emotional responses are linked to the limbic system.

The cells in the middle of the brain have an insulating layer around them called myelin, and the two halves of the brain are joined by the corpus callosum which enables communication between both sides of the brain. At the back and the base of the brain is the cerebellum. This controls some motor skills and the part of the brain you use when you act unconsciously and without consciously planning your actions. If you think about it and break it down, driving a car is quite complicated, yet once you have mastered it, you drive without thinking. This is where the cerebellum is really useful.

All that being said, there have been a number of cases reported where people have still been able to function well with parts of the brain missing or atrophied. One such person is Nishi Shetty, a student on one of my programs. Nishi told me that in 2007 she was driving to work when her car turned over three times at high speed. She blacked out and only regained consciousness two days later. During that time she had been admitted for surgery and had part of her intestines removed and suffered multiple fractures. Months later, Nishi was still suffering from severe migraines. "It felt like there was a ball inside my head that was hitting the walls of my brain." After consulting a neurologist it was discovered she had permanent atrophy, which was not curable and that her brain mass was reduced by half. The neurologist somberly informed her that over time, cognitive and motor functions would diminish.

Nine years later, tests show that there has been no further deterioration and doctors are astonished. All her motor and cognitive abilities are normal. In fact, Nishi feels she has more mind power than many others. She told me that, "life is not the same... it's better!"

It would seem that the brain is not the only seat of your intelligence!

Getting to the heart of the matter

Have you ever heard that expression 'my heart says yes, but my head says no?' Or 'let's get to the heart of the matter?' While our heart is a powerful organ that pumps blood around the body, the ancient Egyptians' beliefs about the heart remain with us today.

The Egyptians believed that the heart, rather than the brain, was the source of human wisdom, as well as emotions, memory, the soul and the personality itself. Notions of physiology and disease were all connected to the heart. In fact, the heart was considered the most important of the body's organs and not removed during the mummification process, while the brain was unceremoniously discarded.

Does the heart think for itself?

While the heart does not contain brain cells, it does contain neurons that make up its own intrinsic system for regulating cardiac function. In 1994, it was revealed that the heart has a complex intrinsic nervous system that is sufficiently sophisticated to qualify as a brain. This brain in your heart has an intricate network of different types of neurons, neurotransmitters, proteins and support cells similar to those found in the brain in your head. This elaborate network means that it can act independently of the brain in your head and can learn, remember, feel and sense. The heart brain also has its own nervous system that operates and processes information independently of the brain or nervous system. Actually, this is important when it comes to a heart transplant in that nerve connections do not reconnect for an extended period of time. However, the transplanted heart appears to be able to function in its new host through the capacity of its intact, intrinsic nervous system.

Scientists used to assume that it was only the brain that sent information and issued commands to the heart. It wasn't until the 1990s that it was discovered that it works both ways. Indeed, research has shown that the heart communicates with the brain in several major ways and acts independently of the brain in your head.

The heart-brain actually sends messages to the head-brain about how the body feels. So if you're upset, angry or excited, these are accompanied by predictable changes in your heart rate, blood pressure, respiration and digestion. It was observed that the heart communicates with the brain in ways that significantly affect how you perceive and react to the world around you. It is as if the heart can speak to and influence the brain, particularly when the heart is 'coherent', a term used by the HeartMath Institute meaning that it is generating stable rhythms. When the heart rhythm is coherent, the body and the brain experience all kinds of benefits including greater mental clarity and intuitive ability.

Research studies have shown that each human heart emits an electromagnetic field, the largest generated by any part of the human body, which extends up to several feet away from the body in a 360 degree radius. The heart is said to be 100,000 times stronger electrically and 5000 times stronger magnetically than the brain. That means your heart literally communicates with the hearts of others in your immediate vicinity! When you feel good, others feel good and conversely, when you're upset it affects those around you too. Energetic interactions possibly contribute to the 'magnetic' attractions or repulsions that occur between people and also affect social relationships.

More recently it was discovered that the heart secretes oxytocin which is often known as the 'love' or 'bonding' hormone. As well as its function in childbirth causing a mother to bond with her child, evidence also indicates that oxytocin is involved in cognition, tolerance, adaptation, sexual and maternal behaviors, learning social cues and bonding. This could also be a reason that the heart is often associated with love and positive feelings.

Research shows that the heart's neurological signals directly affect activity in the amygdala; an important emotional processing center of the brain. The amygdala coordinates various responses to environmental threats. What it does is compare incoming emotional signals with stored emotional memories and makes instant decisions about the level of the perceived threat. Because of its connections to the limbic system it is able to take over the neural pathways activating the autonomic nervous system and emotional response before the higher brain centers receive the sensory information.

Here's something else to consider. In an accident where the spinal cord is completely severed, the person would have no feeling or muscle function from the neck down. The signals from the brain to the muscles are no longer able to be sent as that pathway is severed which means the person is classified as a paraplegic and confined to life in a chair. The strange mystery here is that the heart continues to function and digestion takes place, despite the fact that the brain, the central nervous system, the organ that sends all the signals to make things work, has had its signals cut. What keeps all these organs going below the neck? Supposedly, your heart depends upon signals from the brain to function and yet it too keeps beating. Is there an even greater intelligence at work?

Gut feelings

Have you ever had a gut feeling about a particular person or situation? Well it turns out that the gut is much more than a digestive system. Research has identified that the gut has an intelligence of its own.

If you think of the gut as a tube with food going in one end and coming out the other, then it makes sense that it would require intelligence to be able to find food, move food and decide what to take in or not. It also needs to protect itself and be able to identify safety and danger. And that is pretty much what the gut does.

If you've ever lived with a cat (and I have three) you'll know that they can be very persuasive when they want affection, food or to play. Similarly, the gut brain is constantly communicating with you. Remember a time when your gut was telling you that it has eaten enough food, yet consciously you overruled the message and continued to eat (particularly if it is chocolate in my case).

In times of threat, your gut will kick in to protect you from danger and keep you safe. Actually, the fight or flight instinct comes from your gut. If you've ever experienced 'butterflies in your stomach,' your stomach 'turning,' or you've made a 'gutsy' decision, then those are expressions from your gut.

Do you remember how you felt last time you had a stomach ache? The gut has a huge impact over cognitive behavior and mental state. After all, if you have a colon that is not working, it means you're basically full of shit and full of toxins and that is going to affect your psychology and your behavior.

Your heart, your brain and your gut are all made up of different types of cells. The term 'cell intelligence' was coined by Nels Quevli in 1916 in his book titled *Cell Intelligence: The Cause of Growth, Heredity and Instinctive Actions*. He showed that the cell is a conscious, intelligent being and plans and builds all plants and animals in much the same way that a man builds a house or a highway. The book reasons that the actions and properties of cells are too amazing to be explained by anything else except their intelligence.

Cell intelligence

Let's start by looking at a single-celled organism – an amoeba. Incidentally, the meaning of the word 'amoeba' in Greek means 'to change!'

Amoebas are so small that you need a microscope to see them. They live in water, including lakes, ponds, streams, rivers and puddles. Some can even live in the bodies of animals.

Being a single cell, an amoeba is enclosed in a cell membrane and contains a nucleus that controls its actions, organelles and cytoplasm (fluid within the cell membrane). For feeding, movement and reproduction they use a method called phagocytosis which means an amoeba changes its shape and reassembles itself thereby creating a pseudopod which helps them move around by stretching out and pulling itself within. To eat, the amoeba stretches out the pseudopod, surrounds a piece of food and pulls it into the rest of its body. Organelles known as food vacuoles do the task of digesting and storing it. The useful nutrients are absorbed while anything potentially harmful remains in the food vacuole and is eventually pushed to the surface via the cell membrane. Imagine that a single cell has the intelligence to know what is harmful!

They reproduce by a process called binary fusion which means they can split in half and make two identical new amoebas. Some amoebas protect their bodies by covering themselves with sand grains. Others secrete a hardened shell that forms around them that has a mouth-like opening through which they extend their pseudopods. When water or food is scarce, some amoebas respond by rolling into a ball and secreting a protective body covering called a cyst membrane. They exist in cyst form until conditions are more favorable for survival outside. To all intents and purposes, they respond to current conditions and take decisions to deal with unforeseen difficulties.

According to Brian J Ford's article in MENSA Magazine February 2010, if you were to open a single cell in a red algal colony in a way that leaves the cell walls torn and empty, the neighboring cells sense that something has happened. They then divide to replace the missing cell content which then sets about to realign and restore the cell to its original state.

A single cell takes decisions to deal with unforeseen difficulties! That is pretty incredible!

If you consider the notion of cells and cell intelligence you discover that cells in your liver, for example, reproduce at just the right rate to replace cells lost through wear and tear (so to speak), follicular cells create new hair, bone marrow cells produce new circulating blood cells at a rate of millions per minute. About 90% of this cell activity is invisible to the brain. Granted, you have many different types of cells in your body, however, if an amoeba can construct a stone home with all the skill of a master builder, what are all your cells together in your body truly capable of?

Then there is the phenomenon of cellular memory such as the 47 year old man who received a heart from a 17 year old and was surprised to discover a new liking for classical music. He was later to discover that the donor loved classical music and had played the violin. A woman who loved fast food received a heart from a 19 year old vegetarian and reportedly told nurses following the operation that she felt nauseous at the very thought of eating meat.

Modern science tells you that your cells contain your DNA, the blueprint for the complete design of your physical body. Your DNA is what makes you uniquely you. It's that double helix that your genes are made of and it accounts for why you resemble your parents and it distinguishes you from everybody else. Your cells hold the blueprint for your emotional, mental and spiritual state and your cells remember all of who you are and have been right up to the present day. As you change, grow and evolve in any area of your life, your cells are continuously updating your personal information. Cells also hold the information of all life experiences that may have been absorbed from your ancestors and genetic heritage. You'll discover later on in this book that epigenetics (the study of heritable changes in gene expression) has now proved that you do not necessarily inherit certain diseases from your parents and grandparents and that change can occur.

While not everyone can agree on how cellular memory works, if you look at the world of vaccines and how they work (a touchy subject for many parents) it gives you a clue on how cellular memory works. A vaccine means giving a patient a small amount of unhealthy organisms so that the patient's immune system sets up a defense to protect the patient from becoming ill from that particular illness. So that means the immune system remembers and the vaccine evokes cell memory.

You are made up of 50 trillion cells so basically, you are a community of cells. Dr. Bruce Lipton says that cells respond to two types of signals from the environment. First, cells respond to physical chemicals such as hormones, drugs etcetera. The second type of signal is vibrational energy. In experiments, Dr. Lipton proved that when cells in a petri dish were exposed to a bad environment they became diseased. Instead of treating them chemically in order to heal, he simply placed the cells back into a healthy environment and the cells then healed without a chemical intervention.

Is it time to consider the environment YOUR cells live in? And what about the environment you and your body live in?

When John Mayer sang "your body is a wonderland," he was right. Each cell in your body has a purpose and functions separately and collectively. At times you may feel separate from the rest of the world, and it is this separation that often creates disharmony. Could it be that the tiny world of the single cell mirrors your own and that the single cell could be the root of your own intelligence? Cells constantly grow and die and could be seen as the ultimate reflection of how the universe works. After all, the universe is constantly changing and transforming.

Perhaps there is a greater intelligence at work and available for you to tap into?

Spirals

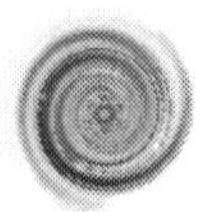

Every second of the day you have over two million bits of information streaming in to your nervous system through your five senses. Your senses take in whatever you experience that you think is outside of you. All this information is filtered through deletion, distortion and generalization. Your filters are unique to you and made up of your memories, life experiences, language, beliefs, values as well as your perception of time, space, matter and energy. This means the way that you see, hear, feel and experience the world is different from how others see, hear, feel and experience the world.

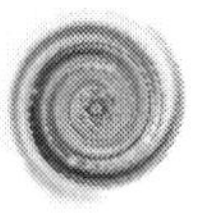

You have the power to choose whether to view yourself as a victim of circumstances or to get into the driving seat and drive your life in a new direction. The world you perceive outside of you is a reflection of your inner world which means there is never a problem with another person, situation or an event. The problem is within yourself and how you choose to perceive that person, situation or event.

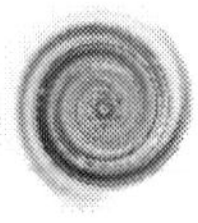

You create and get clear about where you are heading and what you want to achieve with your conscious mind. Your conscious mind is driven by the programs, patterns, habits and behaviors that are running and stored in your unconscious mind.

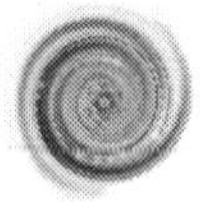

It's estimated that 95% of our decisions, actions, emotions, and behaviors are derived from the unconscious mind which is a powerful information processor that records perceptual experiences and can

forever play them back. So if you want to bring about significant changes in yourself and your behavior, you have to do so at the unconscious level, as well as at the conscious level.

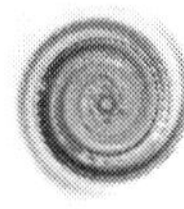

Approximately 100 billion neurons are constantly wiring and firing together so each experience you encounter becomes embedded in the network of brain cells that produce that experience. Each time you repeat a particular thought or action, you strengthen the connection between a set of brain cells or neurons.

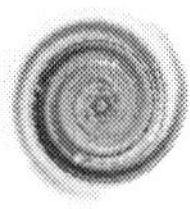

The Egyptians believed that the heart was the source of human wisdom, as well as emotions, memory, the soul and the personality itself. The heart-brain actually sends messages to the head-brain about how the body feels. The heart is said to be 100,000 times stronger electrically and 5000 times stronger magnetically than the brain. That means your heart literally communicates with the hearts of others in your immediate vicinity!

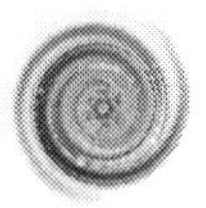

An enormous amount of intelligence is at work within you to run your body from your brain, the 'brain' within your heart, gut intelligence and right down to every single cell in your body. A single cell takes decisions to deal with unforeseen difficulties and your cells hold the blueprint for your emotional, mental and spiritual state. Your cells remember all of who you are and have been right up to the present day. As you change, grow and evolve in any area of your life, your cells are continuously updating your personal information.

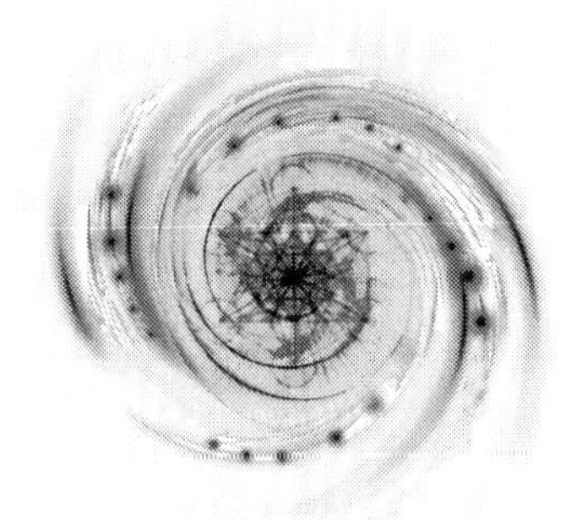

Part Two:

UNLEARNING

"The path to mastery means the letting go of EVERYTHING in your life that represents mediocrity!"

Carol Talbot

It was 3.30am and pitch-black outside. There was a light tap on the hut door indicating that it was time to leave. I was ready except for the rubber boots that are customary footwear in the Ecuador rainforest. Through the quiet of the night we made our way down to the boats and headed through the immense silence that pervaded the Pastaza River as our boat gently and fluidly glided through the waters.

On this particular morning we were joining a family at a small Achuar village for their morning ritual which takes place every day before the sun comes up.

In Western civilization, purging (throwing up through the mouth or diarrhea the other end) is usually considered something to be concerned about. In fact, if you are sick, you take tablets to stop it, or cork it up so to speak! Purging is the body's natural way to eliminate toxins, poisons or stale food that should not be left in the body. And for this reason, it is something that many tribes undertake on a regular basis. All this happens before the sun comes up.

In order to bring about a 'purge,' a tea brewed from plant leaves is drunk. I'm not sure if it was the tea that brought on the purge or the sheer volume of drinking so much, but as I drank to the point where I thought my belly would burst, I rushed from the open air hut and purged every drop out of me.

The dictionary definition of 'purge' is to get rid of something or someone. Incidentally, 'purge' rhymes and contains the word 'urge.' Perhaps you've experienced times when you have a strong urge to purge in order to get rid of or let go of something in your life (or someone) leading to a space clearing. In Latin, purge, or 'purgare,' means to purify or removing impure things, whether that is unhealthy feelings and emotions or stale food in the refrigerator.

I was left with a sense of peace and calm immediately after the purge followed by a wave of new energy washing over me like a refreshing shower as we joined our Achuar family around the fire to share our dreams of the night.

The Achuar tribe is a dream culture, which does not mean that they spend their time sleeping. In fact, once the sun comes up there is much to be done to sustain village life which is the reason they hold great reverence for their visions and dreams. What it also means is that they know you are coming. It is said that you have been dreamed into the rainforest.

Perhaps you have been called forth to where you are now and to read this book. Whether you have, or have not, just remember ***it's often in the 'letting go' that you can reevaluate who you are being, who you want to be and simply allow yourself to BE in the flow!***

Chapter Five:

Unlearning Patterns

"We are what we repeatedly do.
Excellence, then, is not an act, but a habit."

Aristotle

KEY QUESTIONS:

How do you know to be you?

Where do your thoughts come from?

Is it possible to change the habits of a lifetime?

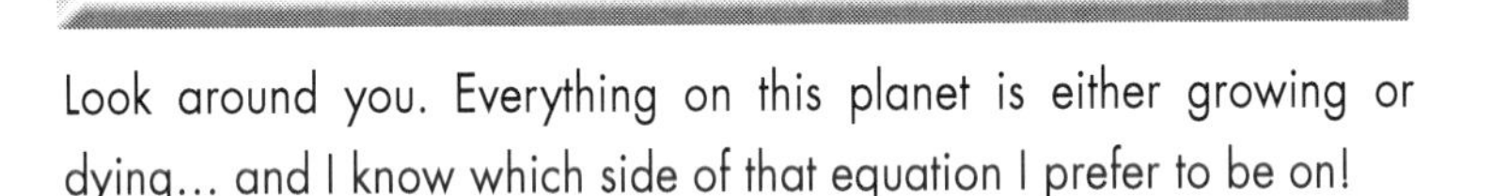

Look around you. Everything on this planet is either growing or dying… and I know which side of that equation I prefer to be on!

On the road of life, whether it is through journaling your experiences be they good, bad or ugly, hiring a coach or mentor, travelling, attending training programs, networking, meditating, reading, watching movies or a documentary, spending time with friends, family or strangers, or out in nature, there is always more to learn and discover!

Every year I make a plan to continually grow and evolve, and attend specific programs or travel to help myself and share the experiences with others. As another year came to a close I looked back through my notes only to find there were very few. Was there nothing new to learn or rather was it me? Had I reached a point where my mind was full and I was no longer open to receiving new experiences?

It was time to stop.

There comes a time when you've learned what you need to learn, achieved what you need to achieve with what and where you currently are in your life. For me, that meant it was time to unlearn.

Learning can be defined as finding the connection between what you know and what you don't know. This is illustrated beautifully in the movie, Dances with Wolves. When Kevin Costner's character first meets the Native American Indians, communication is challenging because neither party can speak the other's language. There's a part where Kevin Costner's character points at a buffalo, enunciating slowing and says, "buf-fa-lo." The Native American Indians also point at the buffalo and say their word for buffalo, "tatanka." When the connection is made between what you know and what you don't know, then learning can take place.

The definition of 'unlearning' then is to 'discard', forget and stop doing something, (such as a habit) in a deliberate way because it is bad or incorrect,' or not getting you the result you want or to where you want to be or go.

I believe unlearning is recognizing patterns in thinking, feeling and behavior that no longer serve you. It's letting go of memories and experience than no longer suit you or fit like a set of clothes you used to wear. Unlearning is letting go of EVERYTHING in your life that represents mediocrity. It's having the courage to say 'no.' It is knowing that you are more, deserve more and are a valuable asset to yourself and others. That is a choice YOU have to make.

So just for a moment, I want you to consider that when you wake up in the morning, how do you know to be you?

It's unlikely that you're wearing a pair of pajamas with your name neatly inscribed on the top pocket, or have a name tag clipped to the bed post.

In those first few seconds of waking what actually happens? Is it the sun streaming through the curtains that wakes you up or is it your bladder that shouts 'I need to pee?' Actually, during the course of a night's sleep, you cycle through five different stages of sleep, from what is considered 'light' sleep to 'deep' sleep and 'REM,' which is when you dream. To prepare for waking up, your body releases a number of stress hormones, such as cortisol. So gradually, your sleep becomes lighter and lighter, and that is when you wake up.

Upon waking, perhaps you reach for your phone, or tap into some memories or look at yourself in the mirror as you make your way to the bathroom. It's as if for a few seconds, you have the opportunity to be anyone you choose! Instead, you lock yourself back into being the person you believe yourself to be with all the memories from your past that allow you to slide back into your particular identity.

I recently experienced a seriously bruised face which no amount of concealer and make-up could hide. It also coincided with a conference I was attending. While I would often forget about my appearance as I immersed myself in the engaging presentations during the conference, the looks from others would draw me back to the fact that I must look like I'd been in a car crash or been beaten up. It is the reflection in the mirror of others and your memories that give you your sense of I-ness.

When you lock into your specific identity, it also locks you into certain patterns, and it's our patterns in thinking and behavior that create our response to circumstances and not the circumstances themselves.

Think of it like driving a car. You first check that the gear is in neutral, and then turn the key in the ignition and that's how you drive a car. If you want flowers to grow in your garden, you need to prepare the ground first and then plant the seeds. Or if you want to call a friend, you need to dial the telephone number in exactly the right sequence in order to connect. And if you've invited friends round for dinner, to produce a gourmet meal, you will need to buy the ingredients first and follow each step of the recipe in the correct order.

Patterns are everywhere and you have a pattern for being you. Once you begin to recognize those patterns you can let old patterns go that no longer serve you or get you the results you want. It's interesting to make a note of what you do every single day and notice the repetition and patterns as well as the results reflected in your life.

Most people know that if they want to be healthy it's about eating the right foods and exercising regularly. Come on, it's not rocket science! Somehow though, it's still easy to get sidetracked by the pizza, burger and chips! That's a pattern of thinking and behavior that would be useful to unlearn if you want to be healthy.

I recently read a report that whales had been beaching themselves in a number of areas. One of the theories around this is that they rely on the magnetic grid system to navigate the oceans, and are deeply affected when there is damage or change to the grid system. In other words, the patterns they have followed in the past have been changed and unless they change too they run the risk of beaching.

If you are creating the same reality every day maybe the patterns for living your life need to change. It's like heading off for a beach vacation, yet your suitcase is still filled with hiking boots and sweaters from your last trip. Or having a map of London when you're going to Timbuktu! So, let's dig deeper into how patterns get set.

In 1902, Dr. Edwin B. Twitmyer (what a wonderful name) submitted a paper to the American Medical Association called "Stimulus Response." It outlined the hammer-to-knee-reflex. You probably know that when someone taps you gently on the knee with a hammer then you get a reflex action and your leg kicks up in the air. What Twitmyer realized was that if he went to tap someone on the knee, even if he didn't actually touch them on the knee, he would still see the knee-jerk reflex action. There was an expectation which created a response. And this is what he wrote about and published. The American Medical Association was not very interested and failed to see its relevance and value at that time.

Dr. Twitmyers' paper was picked up by a Russian physiologist called Ivan P. Pavlov who thought there was something interesting in it and he started experimenting, initially with dogs. What he would do is put some steak in front of them and when the dogs started salivating he would ring a bell. He would do this again and again... put some more steak in front of the dogs, and again, when they started salivating he would ring a bell. He did this so many times that he found that just ringing the bell would make the dogs salivate, even though there was no steak. In his research, he associated the sound of a bell to when the dogs were hungry and would salivate. In 1936, after years of research with dogs, he submitted a paper to the Russian Medical Society called 'Conditioned Reflexes.'

As a human being, you are literally a conditioned response machine. Just consider some of your conditioned responses today. If you have been driving then a red traffic light is the trigger that creates the 'stop' response. If your stomach rumbles that's the trigger that you want something to eat, or if the alarm clock rings in the morning that's the trigger that creates the response of either getting up or rolling over and pushing the snooze button!

These conditioned responses can occur or be created in any of the five senses. For example, any time I smell freshly cut grass I'm transported back to fond memories of my father mowing the lawn. For you it may be the smell of freshly brewed coffee or freshly baked bread that creates an instant response of pleasure. Perhaps someone walks by you wearing a particular perfume or cologne that reminds you of a long lost friend. Or maybe a particular song recreates memories of a great party or vacation.

As well as triggering positive memories, you also have unknowingly created negative responses to specific triggers. Perhaps a person looks at you in a particular way and you feel nervous, or your partner leaves the top off the toothpaste tube again and you get angry!

In fact whenever you respond without thinking, you are under the influence of a conditioned response which makes them a powerful force in your life because they build your habits. Research indicates that 40 – 45% of what you do every day is actually a habit. You may feel like you are taking action and making decisions, when actually the action and decisions you make stem from your habits. While they help you learn to become really good in certain areas, so for example, you don't have to think about stopping for a red traffic light because the red light IS the trigger for stopping, they can also hold you in a pattern of less than useful responses and reactions.

Perhaps you reach for the cookie jar when you are stressed. I know many people reach for something sweet when they are anxious rather than a healthy apple or a plate of kale! Could it be that you were given candy and chocolate when you were upset as a child thus creating a habit of reaching for sugar when you are stressed? That then is another example of a conditioned response.

As it's a learned association that means you can begin to create more useful conditioned responses and release the triggers that no longer serve you. In fact, many phobias begin after a person has had a negative experience. For example, after witnessing a terrible boating accident, a person might develop a fear of the sea. This is an example of a negative conditioned response.

How much are you driven by your unconscious patterns and conditioned responses? Chances are, you've picked up many unwanted patterns from the past which, unfortunately, are still alive in you today. **After all, surely if you were consciously choosing your responses and reactions, you would choose to be happy, joyful, alive and fulfilled.** So it's time to do an audit on your thoughts and discover how your brain is firing.

First, the good news! **You have the ability to change the software in your brain; to literally change the way you think,** and you think in six different ways; you see pictures so go ahead and picture what your partner or best friend looks like. You hear sounds. Can you hear the sound of your friend's voice? Do you have a favorite perfume or can you imagine the smell of freshly baked bread or brewing coffee? Mmm, I love the taste of my mother's lemon meringue pie. What's your favorite food? Can you remember how it tastes? You also have feelings so bring to mind the last time you felt ecstatic. And here is an important one - you talk to yourself inside your head! The question is what are you saying to yourself inside your head?

Your mental pictures, sounds and feelings all have certain qualities. Your pictures have brightness and color, your sounds have rhythm and tone, and your feelings may have a certain texture or temperature. It is through these qualities that you structure your experiences and how you code your experiences.

The mystery is from where your thoughts come.

Even a simple decision to make a cup of tea, or take a shower could be the result of a thought that suddenly appeared as you were reading a book, or finishing a telephone call, at work, driving, walking, in fact, at any moment of any day. Let's say you are driving along heading for the office and out of nowhere, a new thought comes to mind, 'what shall I buy Jan for her birthday?' It's not related to your journey and it is not related to the day ahead. The thought just appeared. So where did it come from?

The thoughts you have are a result of what you sense and receive. The energy giving rise to the thoughts can come about from a whole myriad of different sources, including what you watch on television, what you read in a magazine or newspaper as well as what you talk about on a regular basis with friends. Actually, the media thrives on negativity. These days, social media has a huge influence on your thoughts. And if you watch a particular television series for a few weeks, it's surprising to notice that you end up dreaming about the characters, talking about the series with friends in often heated discussions!

At the end of the day, there is still much debate on where thoughts actually come from. Indian philosopher, guru and poet, Sri Aurobindo said that all thoughts come from the Universal Mind and that your mind is not an instrument but simply an organizer of knowledge. You accept a certain range of ideas based on your affinity and that which is called the self is just an amalgam of thoughts that have been trapped and keep circulating ('I like this; I hate that; I am this kind of a person'). He said that you may receive and express the same thought or idea differently due to variations in individual mental consciousness. And also, 'inspiration slips in when the mind falls silent – not when the mind is making an effort as is commonly believed.'

It's estimated that the average thought only lasts between six to ten seconds, but what I know is that when I'm bothered or upset by something or someone, it's like pushing the repeat button on a music track or movie. I run the experience and the same thought pattern in my mind over and over again. Be honest, if you go to a movie and it's not very good, it's unlikely that you would go and watch it again. Yet that is precisely what you do with your thoughts by running the same thoughts on repeat!

Thankfully, you do exert some power over your thoughts by directing your attention, like a flashlight, to focus on something specific.

When you have a thought, your brain cells communicate with one another via a process called neuronal firing (see Chapter 4). When brain cells communicate frequently, the connection between them strengthens and it creates a pathway. This enables faster transmission, so if you practice hitting a tennis ball or golf ball enough times, it becomes automatic and your neurons wire and fire together.

What that means is that your patterns in thinking literally become embedded in the network of brain cells and each time you repeat a particular thought the connection between those cells becomes stronger and stronger. All well and good if you are running a pattern of positive thinking, but if you are continually sidetracked by poor habits and pessimistic thoughts then you get stuck in a loop. That explains why some people find it so difficult to change. The more the negative thought loops run, the stronger the neural pathways become, and the more difficult it becomes to stop them! Perhaps you remember the old vinyl records. Sometimes they would get stuck in a groove and play the same four notes over and over again until you nudged it along. If you've heard the saying 'stuck in a rut,' now you know the reason it is so true! Let's nudge you along.

It was once believed that the human brain had a relatively small window of opportunity to develop new pathways in a life span, and after that the pathways became carved in stone, so to speak. It's probably the reason you may have heard older people say 'you can't teach an old dog new tricks,' or 'I'm too old to change.' The field of neuroplasticity is opening up to new possibilities on how learning takes place, with the good news being that you *can* teach an old dog new tricks!

So if 'neurons that wire together, fire together' then 'neurons that fire apart wire apart.' What this means is that it is possible to change and that if you want to learn a new skill or even a new way of being, a new neural pathway is created the more you practice. Studies have been performed on plasticity during meditation and have shown that the brain can change based purely on mental training. This, of course, has huge implications for mental practice and its impact on overall wellbeing. Remember the horse taking tourists around the pyramids in Egypt? It is possible to steer the horse in a new direction!

To highlight the mental aspect, Australian psychologist Alan Richardson ran an experiment with a group of basketball players. Dividing them into three groups, the first group would practice for 20 minutes every day, the second group would only visualize themselves making free throws, but no real practice was allowed. The third group would not practice or visualize.

The results were astounding. There was significant improvement from the group that only visualized; they were almost as good as the guys who actually practiced.

Imagine the implications on all areas of your life when you set aside time to mentally visualize and rehearse a new skill. A few years ago I met an interesting scientist in Mexico. She had been in hospital for several months just prior to our meeting. I was surprised because her arms were toned with the muscles well defined as if she had been working out at the gym on a regular basis. She told me that in a way, she had been going to the gym and working out every day... except the gym she was using was in her mind! Hmm, that may be food for thought if you dislike the gym or cannot always get a workout in. You can do a mental workout while you lie back on the sofa!

So neuroplasticity is what makes personal growth and development possible and refers to the brain's ability to restructure itself after training or practice.

John Hagelin PhD, Professor of Physics and Director of the Institute of Science, Technology and Public Policy at Maharishi University says, "It's important to recognize that our body is really the product of our thoughts and we are beginning to understand in medical science the degree to which the nature of our thoughts and emotions actually determine the physical substance and structure and function of our bodies."

The power of your language

Your thoughts are also expressed through your language so it is worth considering what language you use on a regular basis. After all, you have about one million words available to use in the English language and it's unlikely that you are using a million different words each day. Research indicates that the average person uses up to about 20,000 words a day if you are a woman, and probably only 8,000 if you are a man. Well that could be the reason my brother usually responds with only one or two words in an email! What is more, you will also be using the same 100 words on a regular basis to describe your experiences.

Words by themselves actually have no meaning. It is the structure, the context and the process that gives meaning to a word. For example, 'only you can do this now' and 'you can only do this now,' share the same words yet the process is different thereby changing the meaning. Another example would be 'rain is great if you're a farmer and not so great if it's the first day of a beach holiday.'

If I ask you to write down seven words that mean 'communication' to you, chances are that you and I will each have seven different words. There is a possibility that we may have one or two words the same. However, what 'communication' means to me and what it means to you is likely to be completely different.

Your language determines how you structure your reality created by your thoughts. Remember the brown–red experiment in Chapter 1 that highlighted how your language changed your perception of your surroundings? Your language has a huge impact on how you feel. Let's do another experiment, and what I want you to do this time is to say out loud the phrase, 'I am really angry. Totally and utterly angry. I couldn't be angrier if I tried.' Go on and say it, aloud (probably not a good idea if you're in a public place)! Repeat it a couple of times.

Now how does that make you feel? Are you actually feeling angry? Do you physically feel like someone who is angry?

Now I want you to say out loud the phrase, 'I am filled with joy.' And repeat the phrase with lots of conviction and enthusiasm for at least twenty seconds.

Do you feel different from a minute ago? My guess is that you do. So the language you use to yourself and to express yourself in the outside world changes the way that you feel about things and it also changes your feelings.

A demonstration I'll often do with a group is to ask if anyone in the audience has a mild pain or a headache. I ask them to share on a scale of one to ten (one being low and ten being high) the level of pain. So they give the pain a number. Then I ask them to give me three words to describe the pain. And they give me three different words. Without repeating any of the words they have already given me, I ask them to give me another three words to describe the pain. So they give me three more. And then I repeat it again, give me three more words, and three more, and three more. I keep going until they have completely run out of words. Then I ask them, 'By the way, about your headache, what level is the pain now?'

It has always dramatically reduced, and in most cases people tell me that the pain has completely gone.

The point is that it demonstrates that if you do not have the words to describe something, you cannot experience it. It cannot exist. If you do not have the words to describe a feeling, it disappears. At the very least, its intensity is dramatically reduced. That's powerful!

You have the ability to choose and change the language you use every day to label people, events, situations, and circumstances in your life. This is the process of unlearning language and thought patterns. As soon as the label changes, your experience and the perception of the person, the event, the situation or the circumstance also changes.

Your language has a direct connection with your thoughts. The words that come out of your mouth don't happen by accident. They have a direct relationship with the thoughts that are going through your mind at any point in time. The thought is actually used to generate the language that comes out of your mouth. And as your actions are all primarily unconscious, it can sometimes be extremely revealing, to listen to your language and realize what thoughts you are running on a regular basis.

So quite simply, when you change your language, you change your thoughts and vice versa. In fact, you cannot think any deeper than your vocabulary allows you to.

Notice how you describe yourself to others on a regular basis. What words do you use?

"All that we are is the result of what we have thought. The mind is everything. What we think, we become." Buddha

Who do you want to become? Because what you create is expressed in your language, therefore if you change your language, you begin to change your universe, unlearning and letting go of patterns that no longer serve you. Your world literally comes into being by what you create with your thoughts and mind and there are endless possibilities to change reality. And your thoughts, when you run the same thought over and over again become your beliefs!

Chapter Six:

Believe It... or Not!

"Imagine going beyond the boundaries of who you believe yourself to be."

Carol Talbot

KEY QUESTIONS:

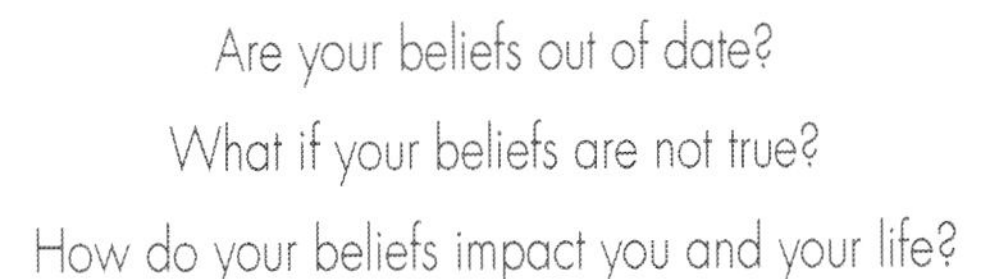

Are your beliefs out of date?

What if your beliefs are not true?

How do your beliefs impact you and your life?

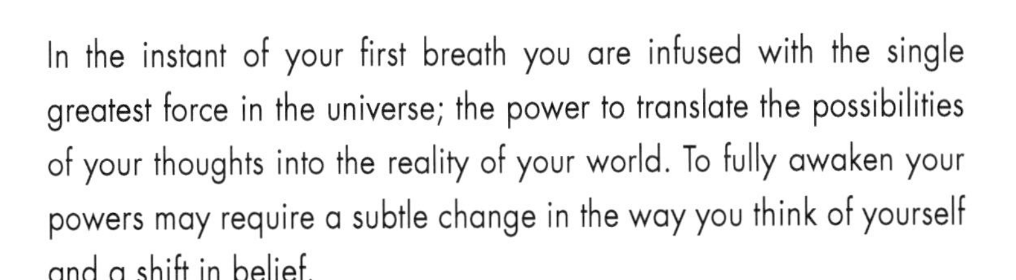

In the instant of your first breath you are infused with the single greatest force in the universe; the power to translate the possibilities of your thoughts into the reality of your world. To fully awaken your powers may require a subtle change in the way you think of yourself and a shift in belief.

Beliefs are those convictions that you hold as being true and trust as being true. Simply put, a belief is a thought that is thought over and over again. What makes a belief true or real is that you have to believe it intellectually, and you have to believe it emotionally. If you only believe the thought intellectually, it is just an idea. If you only believe the thought emotionally, then it is just a feeling. When the belief is held in your thoughts and feelings it becomes true for you. It does not necessarily mean that it is right or even that it is true.

Your beliefs create perceptions that affect your self-esteem, abundance, job performance, mental health, physical health, spiritual outlook on life and your relationships.

When a child comes into the world it comes into a world of possibility with no fear or belief about what is possible or not. Your beliefs are created from your past experiences, from your upbringing, parents, media, schooling, religion as well as your environment. Here's an example of how your beliefs can be created from childhood experiences.

Khaled told me he was moved to tears because of two incidents. The first were tears of joy and the second were tears of compassion and frustration. "I was at a shopping mall on my way for a client meeting when I could feel something suddenly cling onto the side of my right leg. As startled as I was, I noticed what looked like a 7 year old child with glittering eyes of joy and a smile that could light up the sky. 'Habibi!' he exclaimed, as if he had found a lost valuable item. 'You're so big because you have a big heart!'"

"I couldn't believe my ears, and felt a rush of emotion going up to my eyes as they started to well up with tears. He gave me, well, my leg, a big hug and ran back to his family.

Later, after the meeting, I walked back to my car to find a 12 year old boy with his mother in what seemed like 'lecture time.' The boy was already dressed up in basketball attire, while his mother was trying to talk him out of it and said in a strict tone of voice 'well it's not like you're God's most gifted boy anyway. You're short! You don't belong on that basketball court.'

I saw the frustration and disappointment in the boy's eyes that would be shaping his self-image and belief system around what he probably loves. I saw the beliefs of 'I'm not worthy. I'm not deserving' on his face as I walked past him and his mother.

I was struck by the sheer difference between both children because they both told two different stories in the same context: the power of love in whatever way it was communicated. One boy's reality and belief was around giving and self-worth, while another boy's reality and belief was around limitation and unworthiness."

Chances are, you have picked up some worthy and helpful beliefs as a child and it's likely that you also absorbed and created some negative beliefs which may no longer serve you today. Consider the following:

- Do you eat the same food you were given as a baby?
- Do you dress like a 5 year old?
- Are you still riding around on a little toddler tricycle?

Probably not! You grow up into an adult; you learn and constantly evolve and develop yourself which means that you've outgrown certain things. If you change clothes, cars, where you live, your job, your hair style, your relationships and friends then surely it would make sense that you also need to change or update your beliefs. Indeed, are your current beliefs supporting the lifestyle you want or are they sabotaging you and the life you would like to create for yourself?

The power of a belief

No doubt you have heard Henry Ford's saying, 'whether you think you can, or think you can't – you're right!' Your beliefs form the rules that you run your life on for better or worse. Your beliefs are literally behind everything you do whether you know it or not. Your beliefs drive all your behavior and the challenge can be that you are probably not consciously aware of what beliefs are driving you forward... or backward! You just know that certain areas of your life are not working.

Here's a tip. If there is an area of your life that is not working, ask yourself 'what would I have to believe about myself to have my life this way?'

Let's say you have a disempowering belief about attracting a loving relationship. How much effort are you going to put into attracting a loving relationship? Probably not very much and if you are not putting in very much effort the result is likely to be that you don't actually attract loving relationships. That means you have now proved the original belief to be true which in turn makes it stronger and stronger.

A quote on social media caught my eye recently. It said 'growth is painful, change is painful, but nothing is as painful as being stuck somewhere you don't belong.' Whoa! If the belief is that growth and change are painful then that's a person who is going to be stuck in a rut! I believe that growth and change are exciting and that having the courage and awareness to follow your heart is a good thing.

And it is possible to change even a strongly held belief.

Breaking through beliefs

Fire-walking has been practiced on every continent (except Antarctica) and by cultures around the globe for thousands of years. Some cultures use the fire-walk for power and energy, others for healing or a rite of passage, for example from childhood to adulthood. Just for a moment consider the reason this powerful ritual would persist for thousands of years because it's not as if the world needs more fire-walkers. However, what the world does need are people who can face their fears with courage and breakthrough their beliefs of what is really possible. And in that, the fire-walk certainly works!

At my fire-walking events, the first requirement is to sign a mandatory waiver, which states that the fire-walk is a dangerous activity and there is risk of being hurt. Many people are naturally reluctant to sign such a form and perhaps I should add that nobody is ever forced to walk across hot coals against their will. What I find so beautiful to watch and witness are the shifts and changes that occur within people over the course of a few hours. I've seen people move from 'that's impossible' to 'it's possible,' from 'can't do' to 'can do,' and literally dance across the fire in joy! It's a 'blow your mind' experience that shifts the boundaries that have been created in the mind and by conditioning.

The fire-walk does something to the human psyche that helps people overcome limitations internally and externally, shifting reality and beliefs about what is really possible.

The placebo is another example of challenging beliefs about what is possible and highlights the impact your beliefs have over your health. Basically, a placebo is a 'fake pill' that should have no effect on your body. Yet tests and trials have proven again and again that they often work as well as or even better than drugs or surgery. Because the patient is not aware that he is being given a 'placebo' and believes that the actual drug is being taken, it appears that the belief that the drug will work is all that is needed to allow the healing to occur.

In 1957 'Mr. Wright' was found to have cancer. Hospitalized in California, and with large tumors, he had been given only days to live. He heard that a horse serum called Krebiozen appeared to be effective against cancer and decided that was the route for him. Just before the weekend he received his first injection and surprised doctors when, by Monday, he was up and about, joking and laughing with other patients and extolling the healing virtues of Krebiozen. His doctor wrote later that the tumors 'had melted like snowballs on a hot stove.'

The story doesn't end there, because months later, Mr. Wright came across a report that slammed Krebiozen. He subsequently suffered a relapse. Thankfully, his doctor probably advised him not to believe everything that is in the newspapers and went ahead injecting him with 'a newer and improved version of the drug.' Actually, it was water, but who cares because the tumor masses melted once again.

Apparently Mr. Wright was healthy for another few months until he read another report that stated that Krebiozen was ineffective. He died two days later, and that certainly proves the power of beliefs!

That said, an episode on David Suzuki's *The Nature of Things*, shared the example of a woman with very bad irritable bowel syndrome (IBS). In this experiment, the patient was told that she was being given a placebo and yet her IBS disappeared. The placebo still had the same effect even though the patient knew it was just a placebo. Could it be the excitement of expectation that creates what many would call magical shifts?

As it becomes apparent that the placebo effect has tangible results, new techniques of brain imagery and visualization are uncovering a host of biological mechanisms that can turn a thought, belief or desire into an agent of change in cells, tissues and organs. It would seem that human perception is based on what the brain, based on previous experience, believes will happen next. That means that your past could be negatively impacting you now.

No doubt, you have probably created a belief system based on what happened to you in the past. In fact, most people believe that their past is what has created who they are now. This is an example of 'experiences create belief,' when actually it is the other way around. *Beliefs create experience.* Your inner world creates your outer world. The old model of the world was that the past does indeed create the present and the future, however, the quantum world has provided evidence that we live in a series of 'nows!' This means that if you have had challenges or situations that still bother you right now, the problem is in how you are choosing to re-present past experiences in the now. After all, if something happened to you when you were five years old, you cannot go back to being five years old. All you can do is re-present that experience when you were five years old in the now. A shift occurs when you choose to change how you re-present the past now, so that it no longer impacts you negatively. As Mark Twain said, "it's never too late to have a happy childhood!" Your true power lies in the NOW!

In the 1980s, Harvard Professor of Medicine, Herbert Benson and his team of researchers studied monks living in the Himalayan Mountains who could, by using a yoga technique, raise the temperature of their fingers and toes by as much as 17 degrees. Actually, if you speak with women going through the menopause, they will tell you that this is nothing. When experiencing a hot flash, their body temperature rises to the point where you could probably fry an egg on their back! Anyway, I digress. Back to the researchers, who also studied advanced meditators in Sikkim, India, where they were astonished to find that the monks could lower their metabolism by 64 percent. In 1985, they actually made a video of monks drying cold, wet sheets with body heat alone. Monks spending winter nights 15,000 feet high in the Himalayas is also not uncommon.

Creativity, new inventions and technology are continually breaking down the walls of our beliefs about what is possible. I recently read that Danish scientists, working out of the University of Southern Denmark have uncovered crystalline materials which are capable of pulling oxygen out of both air and water, a discovery which could eventually mark the end of the need to carry around cumbersome oxygen tanks. The revolutionary crystalline material can bind and store oxygen in high concentrations, then control its release time depending on what the user needs. This new discovery could even benefit deep sea divers, giving them superhero-like abilities to stay submerged for extended periods of time without an air tank. Now that's a belief shift!

So if your life is based on your beliefs, what if your beliefs are not true?

In the movie, *The Truman Show*, Truman Burbank appears to have an ideal life. Married with a lovely wife he lives in a small town. What Truman doesn't know is that his life is the focus of a reality TV show which has been aired since his birth and he is the star of the show! His hometown is a giant studio set and his friends are actors playing their role. Deep down Truman believes that he is destined for greater things and plans his escape from this small hometown to see the world. In order to do this he needs to face his fear of the sea. When he finally faces his fear to sail away he discovers that the 'horizon' is actually the edge of the studio set. Perhaps your life is like a studio set created through your perceptions and beliefs about the world.

So grab a pen and paper and let's challenge some of your beliefs right now!

List the 9 most important things you believe you should do in life

List the 9 most important things you believe you should not do in life

Look at your responses and ask yourself, '*when* did I learn this and *who* did I learn it from?'

What you will discover is that many of the beliefs of your life are not your own. Many of your beliefs have been learned from somebody else without you even challenging the truth of the belief. Because of this you feel that somehow these beliefs that are limiting you, are no longer your own.

You begin to change them in the moment you recognize them. Imagine turning the light on in a dark room so that you can instantly see what has been tripping you up when you've been walking around. Now the light is on!

Now that you are aware that some of your beliefs do not belong to you, imagine that as you walk in to your home, you are able to check in, at the door, absolutely EVERYTHING in your life that is not working. It's a little like taking your dirty laundry to the dry cleaners, checking it in, and voila, two days later, taking advantage of the home delivery service, your dirty laundry arrives back at your home fresh, clean and pressed!

Instead of checking your dirty laundry in to the cleaners, just suppose you check ALL your beliefs in at the door. It would mean that you walk into a space and place where ANYTHING and EVERYTHING is possible; starting anew where you can truly be a reflection of your perfection of the connection to your true and perfect self!

As you draw yourself to a higher degree of self-awareness you will realize that a lot of your beliefs have been passed down to you from your family and through generations.

What would be some better beliefs to support you on your journey?

Some of my new beliefs include 'I'm always in the right place at the right time,' 'I'm always in the flow,' 'life is magical,' and 'I always love, trust and approve of myself unconditionally.' Once you've decided on some better beliefs, make sure you demonstrate that belief in your behavior to enforce the new belief.

You learn through looking within and when you can recognize yourself as your own creation you then free yourself from the fear of living a less than satisfying life and expand the horizons of your beliefs, stretch your heart, mind and the boundaries of what is possible. Are you ready to let go and enjoy the ride?

Chapter Seven:

Letting Go!

"Tremendous power lies in letting go."

Carol Talbot

KEY QUESTIONS:

Who are you being?

Does your past create your present and future?

Is it time to let your 'story' go?

Just imagine what it would be like if you could see yourself through the eyes of the person you've become?

Albert Einstein believed there is no true division between past and future, there is rather a single existence. However, he was unable to change the temporal mentality ingrained in society. British physicist, Julian Barbour states that the illusion of the past arises because each now contains objects that appear as 'records.' 'The only evidence you have of last week is your memory. But memory comes from a stable structure of neurons in your brain now.'

Let's say you go to an allopathic doctor expecting a prescription of pills or the option of surgery for whatever ails you. He says, 'you've got blank, blank, blank.' If you have no idea what 'blank, blank, blank' is, it holds no meaning for you. He has not said it's cancer, leukemia, a virus or mental disorder. He has just said you've got 'blank, blank, blank.' Actually 'blank, blank, blank' could even be a good thing because you have no frame of reference for it and it is not linked or associated with any memories. If the doctor says 'blank, blank, blank' with an expression and voice tonality of extreme worry and concern you would probably place some meaning in that. If he says 'blank, blank, blank' with a smile on his face you would probably take it in a positive direction. You create the interpretation in the *now*. It is the filter of experience and memory that impacts our expectations in the now and creates meaning for us.

The new model of the world is that everything is created in the 'now,' which means you can transcend time. All you need to do is *change the way you think*, change how you view past events and change your approach to life. That is easier said than done.

People get stuck in their story. Let's say you meet some new friends and they ask about what you do and how you got to where you are right now. You tell them your story. Or if your life is not working and you go for help to a therapist, coach or counsellor, you are going to be sharing your story. The story you identify yourself with gets told over and over again.

If you go and see a presentation, chances are the speaker will share their 'story.' How many times is that presenter sharing the same story, holding them in an endless loop!

When I met Masood, it was over a year since his relationship with his wife had gone into crisis mode due to what he believed to be 'inappropriate behavior'. Since that time, they had been going through individual and relationship counselling as well as each seeking other healing modalities. Every time they went to a therapist they were asked to share their story again which was actually keeping them stuck. I asked Masood about his relationship and how it was going **now**. "It's transformed one hundred and eighty degrees in a positive way and direction," he told me. Every time Masood chose to relate the story of an incident that occurred over a year ago, it created unnecessary stress and angst for himself. The moment he focused on the present, he noticed how happy they were, which led him to *forgive the past and feel gratitude* for a situation that ultimately brought them together in a more fulfilling way.

Please note the importance of forgiveness AND gratitude. Forgiveness by itself creates an imbalance. If you forgive another person it still implies that they have done something against you. When you offer gratitude for the experience, you can then appreciate that the person or situation was created for your own growth and learning. You can then also appreciate that YOU created the opportunity for growth and learning. And it's surprising how the universe answers that call!

It is often crisis that creates evolution. If you ask a sample of entrepreneurs how they got started in business, they will probably tell you they got fired from their job. That's what happened to me! At the time it was not a great feeling yet looking back, it was one of the best things that could have happened to me. And if I'm honest, it had been on my mind and in my thoughts to leave and 'do my own thing.' The universe gave me a nudge.

"Come to the edge," he said. "We can't, we're afraid!" they responded. "Come to the edge," he said. "We can't, we will fall!" they responded. "Come to the edge," he said. And so they came, and he pushed them. And they flew. Guillaume Apollinaire

A few years ago Don felt that he had reached a peak in his career which left him with the question 'what next?' He felt a sense of frustration because he had no idea where to head next and what to do. He felt stuck in the role, title and identity that his qualifications and certificates placed him in.

Unlike Don, and as I look back, I've held many different roles and titles from advertising executive, legal conveyancer, promotional assistant, recruitment consultant, fitness instructor, yoga teacher, marketing manager, trainer, consultant... never trapped into the identity of a specific role or job title. Whenever I got bored, I would simply look around and see who had a job that looked fun and exciting. However, several years back I found myself facing a brick wall with a huge 'what now?' question looming over me.

There was a feeling of angst and a continuous stream of unanswered questions. 'What should I do?' 'Who should I speak to?' 'Should I let everything go and close the business?' 'What do I still enjoy doing?' 'What is my life's purpose?' This frustration created a vibration of being aligned with unanswered questions rather than a vibration of alignment with a solution. My outer world became the reflection of my inner world and the frustration, angst and anxiety manifested in a very painful way.

I woke up on a warm October morning and could not get out of bed. It was impossible to sit up or even roll over onto my side without a sharp pain shooting down my left arm right down to my fingertips. It was the kind of pain that literally knocks the breath right out of you. At first, I was shocked and wondered whether it was just pins and needles or if I had slept in an awkward position.

With considerable effort I got out of bed and thought that a few yoga stretches and spine twists would nudge everything back into place.

Actually, I even went to a yoga class that morning followed by a personal training session at the gym. Since that strategy did not elicit favorable results, next stop was a chiropractor for a couple of clicks, cracks and crunches to realign whatever was misaligned. The next day the pain shouted loudly back at me begging me to look deeper within yet I went to back to the chiropractor and promptly burst into tears.

It's challenging to meditate and look within when you're unable to find a comfortable position; when every micro movement elicits a painful shock. I was not brave. I cried and cried in a way that briefly halted the endless chatter from my dear friend, the conscious mind, who was intent on analyzing what was occurring by bombarding me with a million questions.

One evening, a group of friends from the healing community generously all stepped in to 'blast' me with energy and healing. Later that same evening, one of them took me aside and said 'are you aware that you didn't accept any of the healing?' What! Why on earth would I refuse help and healing when I was in such pain, distress and discomfort? But you know, he was right. I had not accepted healing that evening.

I was holding on tight to an identity of being strong, of being a 'giver' rather than a 'receiver' which incidentally creates an imbalance and dishonors others when they seek to give.

An MRI highlighted 'desiccated discs' in my neck along with trapped nerves. The prognosis and treatment protocol that allopathic doctors dispensed was not appealing and so it was that I finally asked for help from a space and place of 'ready and willing' to receive.

Arms and hands are usually associated with a lack of willingness to embrace life and create your desires, while the neck is connected to flexibility and self-expression. Pain also requires forgiveness.

I refused to identify with either the pain or the desiccated discs. Perhaps you've heard people talk about 'my pain,' 'my illness,' 'my problem' or 'my accident.' Instead, I experimented with many of the tools and techniques from NLP, Time Line Therapy™ and Hypnosis, creating new ways to connect to a deeper level of awareness within. Personifying the pain I spoke to it as well as noticing the language I had been using to describe it and started using powerful and positive language instead. While language is the domain of the left hemisphere of the brain, I used imagery which is the language of the right brain.

Imagination is only possible with intuition and intuition grows stronger when you listen and act on it. Intuitively, I began visualizing a ball of wool being unraveled to literally un-trap the tangle of nerves in my neck. My intuition was spot on here as a few days after creating this image I opened a book that recommended similar imagery.

Just as a machine needs to be oiled, the body, mind, heart and soul require nurturing. The final healing took place several weeks later when I put myself in the hands of two beautiful women who nurtured and cared for me with a daily Ayurveda massage at a retreat center in Kerala, India.

There is always a point and purpose to pain and a strong indicator from the body's intelligence center that your emotional health is out of balance. I believe that the body is designed for self-healing. After all, if you accidently scratch your arm, you think nothing of it knowing that the scratch will be healed and gone in a few days.

The experience certainly accelerated my awareness and empathy for others and allowed me to pay attention and express my emotions more fully. It was a gradual 'letting go' of an old self and while for some it could be perceived as a negative experience, it is often in the negative experiences that you ignite a desire of what you do want as well as opportunities to evolve and grow.

At both the conscious and unconscious level my deepest desire had been to evolve and grow and the universe provided the vehicle and the opportunity for growth... although not in the way I had expected. (Perhaps I should have been more specific about that!).

For Connor, it was a serious accident that allowed him to finally accept his sexuality, who he truly wanted to be and step into a new way of being. I suspect that somewhere along the line you've been told 'you've got to love yourself.' However, no matter how many times you look in the mirror at yourself and say 'I love you,' it doesn't mean that you really do or that your beliefs are supporting that statement. To love and accept yourself for who you truly are, for most people, is a huge challenge. And when you do, and recognize that you are indeed a manifestation of your own creation, that is when you will feel true freedom.

The liberation that Connor experienced after rejecting himself for over thirty years has opened up many other opportunities for him, although members of his family still need a little time to adjust.

Consider yourself as being stuck behind a slow driver. You have the choice to stay behind and go slow too, or you can wait for the right time to overtake. To let go requires a shift in gear and in many ways, a death of the old self to allow for the new.

If you've ever been to a tarot card reader and drawn the death card, you've probably felt apprehensive about the future. It may have brought up one of life's biggest fears; death. Rather than a physical death, the card is more to do with a death of the old self to allow for the new.

Mas Sajady is a hugely popular gifted healer with extraordinary abilities and a huge following. A former computer programmer he went through not one, but two near death experiences which subsequently awakened his intuitive abilities. Of his two near death experiences, he says they were the best experiences he has ever had.

Several factors seem to be common with near death experiences such as a tunnel of light, which many believe to be the portal to the afterlife or other dimensions, feelings of calm, peace and love, and out of body experiences. Medically and scientifically, this has been explained as a product of oxygen and blood supply starvation to the retina. The retina is the light sensitive membrane at the back of the eye. It receives its blood supply from a central point at the back of the eye, and this blood then spreads around to the edge of the retina. That means that the edge of the retina has a poorer blood and oxygen supply than the rest of the retina. When the oxygen supply is depleted the edges of the retina fail so that all you are left with is a single spot of light and science explains that this is the tunnel that people see.

Science also explains that oxygen starvation primarily causes malfunction of the prefrontal lobes of the brain and it is this that causes feelings of calm and happiness. As for out of body experiences, well there is a part of the brain called the angular gyrus which when activated by disease or electrical current such as during surgery, can cause out of body experiences.

For neurosurgeon Eben Alexander these were the hardcore facts explaining near death experiences. Then his own brain was attacked by a rare illness. In his case, the part of the brain that controls thought and emotion shut down and Alexander lay in a coma for a week. Then, he suddenly opened his eyes and subsequently became a medical miracle. His journey during those seven days in a coma is even more remarkable. Prior to his illness he had no belief in heaven, God or even the soul. He says that he was guided into the deepest realms of existence to the Divine Source of the Universe and today, he is a doctor who believes that death is not the end; it is a transition. His story is shared in his hugely popular book, *Proof of Heaven*.

It seems that to manifest a 'wake-up call,' dis-ease (I mispronounce that purposefully), accidents, crises or near death experiences are often the catalyst for major identity shifts (although one of my clients simply lost his passport).

You don't need to create a near death experience, trauma, drama or disease to create an identity shift or let go of unwanted beliefs. However, be aware that if you're calling out for wealth or abundance, the universe may deem that first you need to experience a lack of wealth or poverty to truly understand wealth. To understand love perhaps you need to understand its opposite. Often it is the negative experiences that call forth a desire and intention for something better and in doing so allow for growth.

In Indian philosophy, there are three qualities that apply to everything in the universe from matter to thoughts, emotions, and states of consciousness. These three gunas (attributes and qualities) are called:

- Sattva which is about starting things, goodness, constructiveness, harmony and linked to who you are being.
- Rajas represents change, passion, activity and what you are doing.
- Tamas represents stopping and bringing things to completion, darkness, destructiveness, chaos and is linked to what you are having in life.

All of these three gunas are present in everyone and everything. It is the proportion that is different, according to the Hindu worldview. If you want to be 'doing' something different or 'having' a different result in life, it starts with changing who you are choosing to 'BE.'

If you are 'BEING' the person who is unlucky in life, then that will affect what you do and what you have. If you are 'BEING' the person who does not know what to do, then that will affect what you have. And if you are 'BEING' the person who is unhappy, then that will be reflected in what you do and ultimately what you have and get.

Indeed, Connor embraced his true self while Mas, and Eben both let go of an outdated model of the world. It does not mean that their lives are totally nirvana; however they no longer need the drama because they have seen a bigger perspective. In acknowledging a bigger perspective all of them have transformed themselves and others in a way which allowed them to completely shatter their beliefs about reality, the world and the universe... and step into a new way of BEING.

So let's suppose that you are reading this in a room with no windows tucked up in bed with a hot water bottle, a heavy duty blanket and a cup of hot tea. Outside there is heavy snow with temperatures of minus 30 degrees. Great if you love skiing or have a snowmobile! A couple of months later, the sun is shining, the trees are blossoming and you are once again in a room with no windows. How do you feel about it when you have no connection to the external environment except what you have been told? You probably feel lousy and depressed when you've been told it's freezing outside while you feel a sense of excitement when you hear about the first blooms of spring. Your response is based on what you have been taught or told.

Now consider the 'world' that you have created for yourself is based on what you have learned, been taught or read or have seen (and now you can understand the part the media plays in creating your world). The 'room' you have created for yourself is based on your memories and past experiences, perception and filters. It's time to let go of the walls that your current model of the world has kept you in. It's time to expand your world. After all, if spiritually enlightened souls can pass through walls, why can't you?

Are you ready to open the door and if so, I invite you to fully consider these questions:

1. Who are you?
2. Who wouldn't you be if you weren't you?
3. What wouldn't you be if you weren't you?
4. What wouldn't it be like to not be you?
5. Where wouldn't you be if you weren't here?
6. Who are you now?

You are living in new times and new energy which is calling for a new way of being. It is time to let your old self die to allow an expansion of your universe and to step forward into a new way of BEING.

Spirals

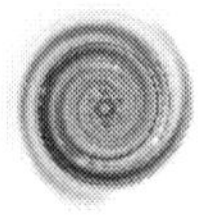

If you are creating the same reality every day then unlearning is recognizing patterns in thinking, feeling, behavior and conditioned responses that no longer serve you, and being prepared to let go of everything in your life that represents mediocrity.

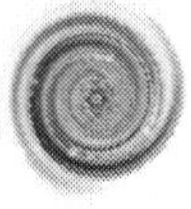

You think in six different ways inside your head (pictures, sounds, feelings, taste, smell and your inner voice). The average thought only lasts between 6 –10 seconds so if you feel bad for longer than that, it means you must be doing something inside your head to continue to feel bad. You do exert some power over your thoughts to re-direct them and in particular how you express your thoughts through language.

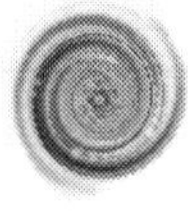

Your thoughts are expressed through your language and you have the ability to choose and change the language you use every day to label people, events, situations, and circumstances in your life. This is the process of unlearning language and thought patterns. As soon as the label changes, your experience and the perception of the person, the event, the situation or the circumstance also changes.

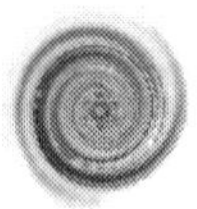

Many of the beliefs that your behavior is driven by were adopted when you were a child which means it is likely that they are out of date. It is also likely that many of the beliefs that you operate and create your life from are not your own. They may have been adopted from your family, culture or heritage. If the belief that a placebo will work can create a return to health it opens the door to the possibilities available when you are operating from powerful beliefs.

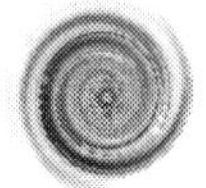

The story you identify yourself with gets told over and over again and holds you in a series of repeated patterns. Like being in a room with no windows we base our lives on what we have been told, taught and through our memories. It's time to create a new identity that expands your current perception of you and your you-niverse.

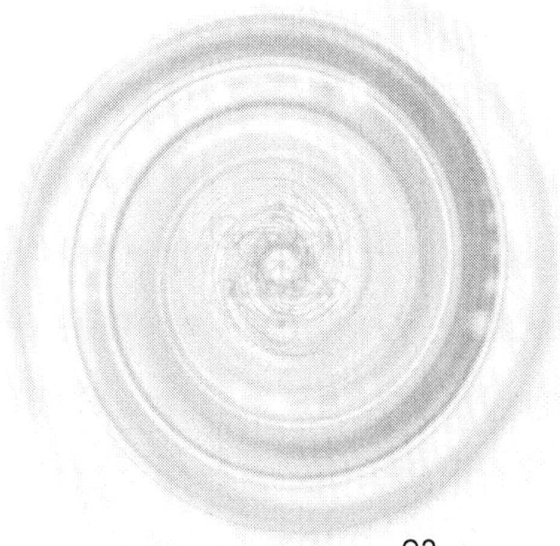

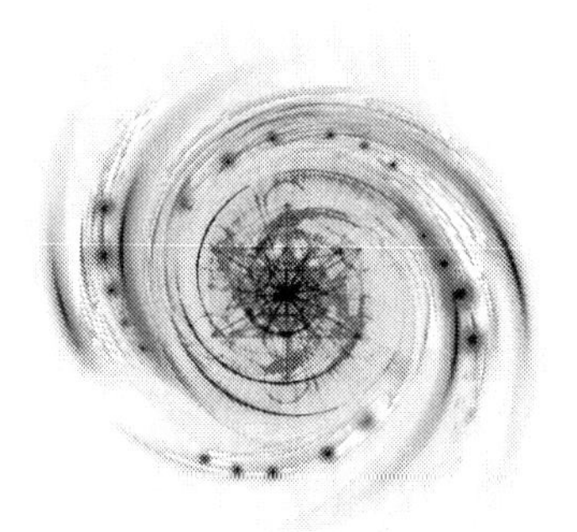

Part Three:

EXPLORING

"Exploration leads to a life filled with fulfillment."

Carol Talbot

Introduction

All the other groups had left Kapawi Lodge earlier in the day to hike in the rainforest with their guides before spending the night with shamans located in different areas of the rainforest. The smallest of all the groups, there were just six of us with no idea of where we would be taken and the pathway there.

To prepare for our meeting with the 'vine' later that night, we had fasted since early morning and now waited with an air of anticipation and trepidation that is usual when you're not quite sure of what you're getting yourself into.

What we did know was that somewhere along our path we would be left alone in the rainforest. Completely alone!

What about dangerous animals, snakes or bugs, you may be thinking and I know I had considered my dislike of such creatures prior to this trip... and booked anyway. Surprisingly, we saw very few animals during our time in the rainforest. It's as if they know you are there and have no desire to meet you either. A silent agreement that worked very well for me!

Our guide was an Achuar tribesman called Diego who spoke his tribal dialect as well as Spanish and a smattering of English. As we went deeper into the rainforest, one by one, he stopped and indicated to another member of our group to leave and sit alone and in harmony with the surroundings. I smiled when Diego stopped and indicated the place where I was to contemplate my very being and connection with all that is. The place chosen was beneath a huge tree with its roots clearly displayed above the ground… and connected to another huge tree. It was as if these two trees were holding hands. Of course the trees in the rainforest are intimately connected both above and below the ground yet the irony did not miss the mark as I realized my time alone was not only to connect with the trees and the earth; it was time to connect with myself. In the middle of our world I was being gifted time to explore the connection to all that is and the nature of reality. Now that's huge!

Chapter Eight:

How to Stop the World!

"The solution will appear when you transcend the level where the problem appeared."
Carol Talbot

KEY QUESTIONS:

Why is it useful to access different states of consciousness?

How can you access different states of consciousness easily?

How do you expand your awareness?

Back in the 1960s, anthropologist and author Carlos Castaneda was interested in altered states and seeking real pathways to other worlds. Now before you assume that he was busy smoking weed, his many books describe his training in shamanism and are based on his experiences under the guidance of a Yaqui, 'Man of Knowledge,' and Shaman called Don Juan Matus.

According to Don Juan, if you really want to access other worlds you simply need to **STOP THE WORLD!** Is that even possible?

Stopping the world is about stopping all the self-chatter going on inside your head so you can have a direct experience of what is really going on. The degree to which you are talking to yourself is the degree to which you are removing yourself from what is really going on in and around you. Similar to experiencing an event behind the lens of a camera: there is a detachment and dissociation from the event itself. Your self-talk also removes you from your senses as you are busy in your own head talking to yourself, interpreting the event or analyzing, criticizing and judging what is going on rather than being present in the moment.

Imagine that as you come into this world you unknowingly create a protective cover around yourself that keeps you safe. Think of this protective cover as similar to the 'room with no windows' that I wrote about at the end of the last chapter. While the protective cover keeps you safe, the cover also keeps you separate from connecting with other people and the world around you. What you then see and experience is your own reflection bouncing back at you from the walls of your cover. Your world is a waking dream of your projection. The first step then is to remove the boundary you find yourself in. It's like a glass of water. The water is contained within the glass and when you shatter the glass the water becomes part of all that is. When you remove the boundary you have put around yourself and your perception of the world, then you can have a direct experience of what is really out there.

The first thing to being present and to 'stop the world' is to quiet the incessant chatter inside. There is a way to do this when you understand brain wave cycles.

Brain wave cycles

All your thoughts, emotions and behaviors create communication between neurons within your brain. Brainwaves are produced by synchronized electrical pulses from masses of neurons communicating with each other and are divided into bandwidths to describe their functions. Think of it as a continuous spectrum of consciousness - from slow, loud and functional, to fast, subtle, and complex.

Brainwaves are like music. Certain notes are similar to a low, rhythmic, pulsing drum while the higher frequencies are like a flute or whistle. It is a symphony that brings all these notes and instruments together.

Your thoughts, emotions and what you are doing impact brainwaves. If you are tired or relaxed, your brainwaves will be slower, and conversely, when you're hyper and buzzed up, your brainwaves will be faster.

Gamma is said to be the fastest of brain waves and relates to simultaneous processing of information from different brain areas. Oscillating within the range of 25 – 100 cycles per second (brainwave speed is measured in hertz and cycles per second), Gamma are the most subtle of the brainwave frequencies as the mind has to be quiet to access these frequencies. Gamma used to be dismissed as 'spare brain noise' until researchers discovered it was highly active when in states of universal love, altruism, and the 'higher virtues.' Experiments on Tibetan Buddhist monks have shown a correlation between transcendental mental states and gamma waves.

A 2004 study took eight long-term Tibetan Buddhist practitioners of meditation and, wired up and using electrodes, monitored the patterns of electrical activity produced by their brains as they meditated. The researchers compared the brain activity of the monks to a group of people new to meditation. In a normal meditative state, both groups were shown to have similar brain activity. However, when the monks were told to generate an objective feeling of compassion during meditation, their brain activity began to fire in a rhythmic, coherent manner, suggesting neuronal structures were firing in harmony. Think of Gamma like an orgasm in the brain, an explosion of sorts that opens up a gateway to expanded consciousness, spiritual growth and a spiritual high.

Remember those times when you've been so absorbed in what you are doing, maybe painting, singing, cycling (and at this moment, for me it's writing), and in those moments time, people and places just seem to disappear. Gamma then, is associated with being 'in the zone.' The key is finding what you love and doing what you love. As easy as this sounds, many people seem to have a challenge feeling comfortable doing what they love and turning it into a business or feel uncomfortable charging a fee for what they love to do and do easily. My view is how can you fail when you are passionate and love what you do? It creates a certain energy and vibration that is infectious and impacts you and others positively.

This reminds me of Muriel. As soon as I met her, I could see she had style and she loved to shop! Life and love had meant that she had enjoyed a lifestyle that allowed for a beautiful home, expensive cars, clothes and possessions. A long drawn out divorce with ongoing animosity meant that what she had previously valued and enjoyed were no longer available. For the first time in her life, she needed a job.

Initially, Muriel thought I was joking when I said 'you're a natural stylist and you love to shop. Create that as your business.' I bumped into her a few weeks later at a networking event and she not only looked fabulous, her energy had shifted from the depressed woman I had met a few weeks earlier. Like trying on a dress, Muriel had put on a new identity... and slipped into her zone! The power of Gamma!

The normal waking state for many people most of the time is known as Beta and it's around 13 – 40 cycles per second. In this brain wave cycle, attention is focused on cognitive tasks in the outside world. It is associated with 'fast' activity, present when we are alert, attentive, engaged in problem solving, judgment, decision making, and engaged in focused mental activity such as reading, working on a computer or glued to your mobile device. In Beta, the outer world is more important than your inner world. It's not a very efficient way to run your brain, particularly if you are continually in the higher ranges of brain wave cycles. In fact, it takes a tremendous amount of energy.

Different information is available at different brain wave cycles. Beta offers you access to a very narrow bandwidth of information which means that you'll not see the wood for the trees! I remember speaking at an event for about 100+ delegates for a multinational organization. At one point during the session I moved in to the audience to speak with one of the audience members. I was standing right in front of him with a microphone in hand and the whole audience focused on this one person. He was so busy on his mobile device, he was neither aware that I was standing right in front of him or that the whole audience was looking at him. Beta can often mean that you 'miss the boat' and miss what is really going on around you. This is what a magician will use to distract your attention. If you've watched an expert magician, they will utilize people's focus to great effect, perhaps making a playing card vanish or other sleight-of-hand tricks.

It makes sense to slow your brain waves down to Alpha. This is one of the most resourceful states in terms of learning and taking in a lot of information without feeling stressed. At around 9 – 14 cycles per second, in this brain wave cycle you feel chilled, relaxed and reflective. The more you slow things down, the more you notice patterns giving you a different perspective on situations. It's as if you are seeing a bigger picture. It is the resting state for the brain helping your overall mental calmness, alertness and learning. And Alpha allows you to access 'the power of now' and being here, in the present.

Theta brainwaves occur most often in sleep, when you're drowsy and are also prevalent in deep meditation. When you slow your brainwave cycles down you are privy to information that only happens when you are in that brain wave cycle. Theta can be the gateway to memory and for many people, they cite mystical experiences during this very slow brain rhythm. It is here that your senses are withdrawn from the external world and focused on what is going on inside.

Scientists have discovered that Theta brain frequency alleviates stress, reduces anxiety, facilitates deep relaxation, improves mental clarity and creative thinking, reduces pain, promotes euphoria, and provides access to instant healings. Not bad, eh? It is often believed that in this state you are able to work directly with Source, Spirit, the Universe, God or Creator of All That Is and facilitate powerful healings for yourself and others.

Theta is the state you are in just as you drift off to sleep. You can access the dream world: imagery and information that is usually beyond your normal conscious awareness.

Theta is often the state produced in a 'shamanic journey,' originally practiced by the indigenous people of far northern Europe and Siberia. The word 'shaman' can be translated as 'the one who sees' or the one who sees in the dark.

It operates from the premise that there is a visible world that we experience through our five senses, and the rational mind. There is also an invisible world of spirit and energy which can be accessed through meditation, trance and contemplation.

I had come across shamanic practices during my initiation path with fire-walking, as well as journeys in South America. However, it was during an extraordinary astrology reading with Michelle Karen that the discussion sidetracked to Shamanic Journeying as a powerful tool to tap into the different wisdom available from the Lower World, the Middle World and the Upper World. I was told that the Lower World is to connect with the soul, ask about past lives and connect with your spirit animal. The Middle World is about the here and now and useful to find something that you've lost or connect with solutions, while the Upper World is a place to meet guides and masters as well as your own future. Specific pathways have been created into these three 'worlds' and your journey is usually accompanied by a rattle or fast, repetitive rhythmic drumming. The drumming or rattle quickly guides you into a trance state facilitating shamanic techniques such as journeying, divination or shapeshifting. When the rhythm of the drumming or rattle changes, it signals that it is time to return from your journey back to the waking state.

Always up to experiment, I have found Shamanic Journeying a quick (15 to 30 minutes), rapid way to gain insights and access wisdom to specific questions. It literally takes seconds to travel to each world once you are familiar with the specific pathways and I usually follow a journey with automatic writing.

Automatic writing, also called channeled writing or inspired writing, is a term to describe the process whereby a person becomes a medium, or channel, for a consciousness that is beyond the individual's awareness.

There are people who claim their hands and fingers are taken over by a spirit and that the pen they're holding basically moves by itself and the words or symbols or doodles that result are from a source separate from their physical selves. This type of automatic writing is the more rare variety. For the vast majority of people, the process of channeled or automatic writing must be initiated by them. In other words, you don't sit there waiting for the pen to move across the page, because you'd be sitting there a very long time. Instead, you actively begin the writing process and attempt to let the words flow without your conscious mind getting in the way with criticism and judgment.

It's fun and enlightening. All you do is relax, perhaps when you've just completed a meditation or shamanic journey, put pen to paper and write, and write, and write with no judgment whatsoever for a specific time period. I suggest you start with five minutes and increase to twenty minutes. You can use a question, photo, quote or wisdom card (you know the ones where you pick a card and it has a beautiful image or wise quote) as a prompt.

Another method is to imagine that you are talking to someone else, someone much wiser, and ask them questions. The answers are the first thoughts that enter your head. Write them down, with no judgment and then expand on them. Just let it flow, no matter how ridiculous or silly it might seem.

Once you feel more confident, perhaps tackle some of the challenges you're facing in life by asking questions then 'downloading' answers. For example, 'how do I get out of this awful job?' or 'for what reason do I blow my diet every night?', or 'what's my purpose in life?' or 'what would make me happier?'

There's no limit to the subjects and questions you can apply automatic writing to, and the idea is that if you really unleash your mind and let it search for new information, you might just shake yourself out of old patterns and behaviors.

Back to brain wave cycles and different states, slowing the brain wave cycles still further, you have Delta. For most people this is a state of sleep and dreaming. You've heard the expression 'you'll feel better after a good night's sleep,' well, healing and regeneration are stimulated in this state, and that is why deep restorative sleep is so essential to the healing process.

Delta is the state of being timeless, formless and linked to states of suspended animation. Deep-level Yogi Adepts can slow their breathing and heartbeat to be virtually undetectable. People are especially open to out of body experiences, astral travel, connecting with spiritual beings, E.S.P., and other phenomena in the Delta brainwave range.

Interestingly, if you consider the states you cycle through as you grow, then in the womb you are naturally in Delta, absorbing patterns and behaviors from your mother. As a young child, you are in Theta and walking around like a sponge absorbing all the beliefs and patterns that are displayed from those around you without judgment. As you grow older you spend more time in Alpha and then as an adult, as I mentioned earlier, your focus moves more into the outside world as we spend more time in Beta.

Any process that changes your perception changes your brainwaves; and it also works the other way around. If your brain wave patterns change then your experience will change.

Chemical interventions such as medication or recreational drugs are the most common methods to alter brain function. A more natural way would be meditation, music and brainwave entrainment. Or here's another way to easily and effortlessly access a slower brain wave cycle and 'stop the world.'

Foveal versus peripheral vision

When you look at an object, the light from that object enters your eyes through the pupils. The iris then changes the size of the pupil, depending on how bright the light is. The light is then focused on the retina which is a mass of light-sensitive neurons, called photoreceptors, which change light signals into electrical ones. The retina is directly connected to your brain and has two types of receptor cells called cones and rods.

The center of gaze, called the fovea, has a higher density of cones than anywhere else on the retina. Foveal vision is used for examining highly detailed objects, the finer distinctions and noticing color differences. It limits the visual field to detect detail.

Rods are the visual receptors which are more highly concentrated toward the outside of the retina. They respond to light at low levels. Activation of the rods in the outside of the retina is called peripheral vision which is used for organizing the wider scene and for seeing large objects. It is also related to the detection of movement, outlines, and night vision.

In Chapter 3 you discovered that it is your unconscious mind that runs your body and your autonomic nervous system (ANS) which regulates the functions of your internal organs such as the heart, stomach and intestines. The ANS is divided into three parts:

The sympathetic nervous system

The parasympathetic nervous system

The enteric nervous system

If you're walking around a park and a large dog rushes up to you and barks then it is your sympathetic nervous system that kicks into action creating the fight or flight/'get me out of here' response. Whenever you are feeling anxious, nervous, fearful, angry, frustrated, irritable, excited, exhilarated or 'pumped-up,' you are in fight or flight mode. *Foveal vision* is hard-wired and connected to the *sympathetic nervous system.*

Back to the park again and this time it's a warm, sunny day and you sit down on the grass, relaxing and enjoying the peace and quiet. This calls for a 'rest and digest' response. Your parasympathetic nervous system is at work to save energy so this is when your blood pressure may decrease, pulse rate can slow, and digestion can start.

Peripheral vision, the relaxation response, is directly hard-wired to the *parasympathetic nervous system* blocking the fight or flight response. In fact, it's impossible to feel a negative emotion when you're in peripheral vision and connected to your parasympathetic nervous system. It activates your relaxation response thereby dropping you into the brain wave frequency of Alpha.

In Hawaii, the Kahuna (Hawaiian title for a shaman) called this prized state of entering into peripheral vision, Hakalau. The process consisted of learning how to enter into a deep trance while maintaining a heightened external awareness.

One of the quickest ways to experience peripheral vision, drop into Alpha and 'stop the world' is to:

1. Pick a spot on a wall where you need to move your eyes up slightly (think of moving your eyes up in the direction between your eyebrows or to the middle of your forehead).
2. As you focus on that spot, pay attention to the peripheral part of your vision. Keep focusing on a spot and expand your awareness, allowing your mind to calm down as you continue to focus on that spot, softening your gaze.
3. Notice that breathing begins to slow down and your mind immediately becomes calm. Continue to expand your awareness...

This will give you an experience of peripheral vision and of course, you would not want to hold your eyes up for too long otherwise you'll experience eye strain.

Now you can 'stop the world,' slow your brain wave cycles and expand your awareness of the world.

Another way to access the Alpha state is through sound (and there is more on sound in Chapter 12). In 1839, Prussian physicist and meteorologist, Heinrich Wilhelm Dove discovered that when signals of two different frequencies are presented separately, one to each ear, your brain detects the difference between the frequencies and tries to reconcile that difference. Basically, when you hear the two frequencies through stereo headphones, they merge in and out between the two frequencies and your brain creates its own third signal, called a *binaural beat* which is equal to the difference between those two frequencies.

For example, if a frequency of 100 Hz is presented to your left ear, and a frequency of 105 Hz is presented to your right ear, your brain 'hears' a third frequency pulsing at 5 Hz, the exact difference between the two frequencies.

Research has proven that introducing a binaural beat will cause the brain to begin resonating in tune with that beat. By creating a binaural beat at an Alpha frequency you can trigger your brain to resonate at that same frequency, automatically inducing brain activity in the Alpha range. This same technique can be used to quickly and easily guide your mind into any state.

Recommended websites for binaural beats include Holosync and Hemi-sync and there are now a number of apps available for your smart device with binaural beats.

Remember, different information is available at different brain wave cycles and peripheral vision will allow you to drop quickly into Alpha or Theta, quiet the continual chatter in your mind and 'stop the world.' You can then access clear guidance from within yourself on how to move forward from moment to moment. And it is guidance you could never figure out in Beta, the state of normal waking consciousness.

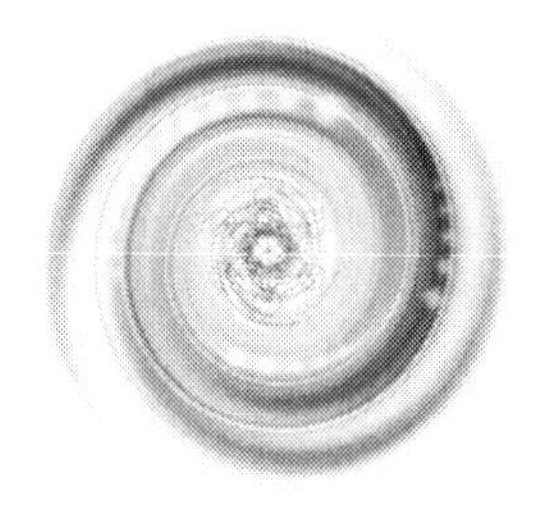

Chapter Nine:

The Power of Trance States

"Becoming 'awake' involves seeing
our confusion more clearly."

Chögyam Trungpa Rinpoche

KEY QUESTIONS:

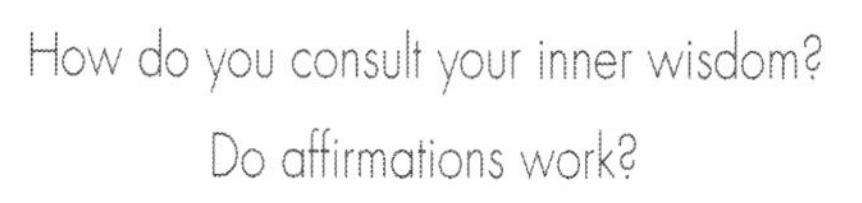

How do you consult your inner wisdom?

Do affirmations work?

What happens between lifetimes?

If there are past lives, could there be future lifetimes to explore from where you are now?

Albert Einstein estimated that we probably use less than ten percent of our brain. Altered states can connect and allow you to access different information and connect to the wisdom stored at the unconscious level.

Researchers speculate that even primitive hunter-gatherer societies may have discovered meditation and its altered states of consciousness simply while staring into the flames of a fire. Across time, people have tried to contact the infinite intelligence and power that lies latent within our very selves. This intelligence has been referred to by many names: Source, God or gods, subconscious mind, higher self, unconscious mind, superconscious... and many others.

The Merriam-Webster dictionary defines meditation as 'the act or process of spending time in quiet thought.' Over thousands of years, meditation has evolved into a structured practice with some of the earliest written records of meditation coming from the Hindu traditions of ancient India with other forms of meditation developing in Taoist China.

In Greece there were the sleep temples where dreams became directly associated with healing. The priests in the Egyptian sleep temples, also known as dream temples, were known to use trance states. Repeating incantations and prayers to answer questions or find solutions to particular problems, the dreamer would then enter the sleep temple and the dreams that came to him would provide the answer. Perhaps you've also found answers, solutions and insights while you sleep and dream.

In the early 1800s, a Scottish eye surgeon named James Braid, having seen trance-like states in a public performance by the travelling Swiss magnetic demonstrator Charles Lafontaine, set out to disprove that eye-fixation causes trance, only to find that it did! In fact modern hypnosis owes its appearance to the investigations made by Braid although he referred to it as 'neurypnology' and that name did not stick. The name 'hypnosis' did!

After James Braid's new research into hypnosis during the 1840s and 50s, scientists around Europe began experimenting with the process in ever greater numbers until the first school of hypnosis was set up by Ambroise Liebeault and Hippolyte Bernheim. Prominent figures such as William James, often referred to as the grandfather of modern psychology, and Sigmund Freud were said to have attended The Nancy School of Hypnosis.

Auto-suggestion

No doubt you have heard the affirmation 'every day in every way I'm getting better and better.' Another influential figure in hypnosis around the turn of the 20th century was the French pharmacist turned hypnotherapist, Emile Coué. He operated his own pharmacy in a small French city, and noticed the strong effect of placebos and positive suggestions, observing that people seemed to heal faster when he sang the praise of a certain medication or left a positive note reminding the patient of the dosage.

In his book *Self-Mastery Through Conscious Autosuggestion*, he says, "autosuggestion is an instrument that we possess at birth, and with which we play unconsciously all our life."

Positive language and positive affirmations are great if your beliefs support the affirmation and what you are saying. If you cast your mind back to Chapter 3, you'll recall that 'all learning, all behavior and all change is the domain of the unconscious mind.' Affirmations target the conscious level of your mind so if your affirmations are along the lines of 'I can accomplish anything I set my mind to,' or 'my body is fit and healthy,' it is all well and good if your beliefs support the statements. If not, then your inner critic or, as I like to call it, your 'oh shit' voice is likely to step in and refute and debunk those statements with 'well, you failed to achieve the last goal you set,' or 'you have to work out every day at the gym if you're going to be fit and healthy.' The good news is that if you find your 'oh shit' voice rejecting an affirmation then thank it because it is actually bringing up the fact that you still have some issues to deal with to create a new and more powerful belief to support your affirmations.

At the turn of the 20th century, Milton Erickson would go on to change the face of hypnosis. He said, "patients are patients because they are out of rapport with their own unconscious. Patients are people who have had too much programming; so much outside programming that they have lost touch with their inner selves." And I believe that remains very much true to this day. He went on to explain that all he really did was to facilitate the state where his patients could get back into rapport with their own unconscious wisdom within.

Just imagine having your very own oracle within to consult with anytime you choose! Perhaps you've heard the whisper of your very own oracle (call it intuition, if you like) and unfortunately, those very whispers are often ignored.

Hypnosis works by partially suspending the constant self-chatter that you may have experienced when meditating. Using vague and abstract language patterns, the conscious mind becomes partially suspended allowing more direct communication with your unconscious mind and allowing you to tap into the wisdom within. It's the key that unlocks the door into your thoughts, memories, emotions and so much more that is stored at the unconscious level of the mind. Remember, your unconscious mind is more powerful than any computer and stores *everything* you take in through your five senses.

You might be surprised to know that you spend the majority of each day in a trance state. It's the most natural state to be in. Perhaps you've experienced the 'driving trance' when you suddenly realize you've arrived at your destination without being fully aware of how you even got there.

Past lives

Exploring trance states further, the late Dolores Cannon's career as a hypnotherapist led her to specialize in past life regression in a career that spanned almost 50 years. Her vast range of books include accounts of when she first discovered reincarnation and how she went on to develop and refine her own unique method of hypnosis known as Quantum Healing Hypnosis Technique (QHHT).

Whether you believe in past lives or not, research shows that 85% of humanity is involved in some sort of spiritual system that does believe in the afterlife. Past life regression is a technique that uses hypnosis and the trance state to recover what practitioners believe are memories of past lives or incarnations. "If you've ever wondered why you have a fear of heights or look into the eyes of a stranger and feel as if you know them, the answers may be found in your past lives," says Brian Weiss, MD, the author of *Miracles Happen*.

Through past-life regression, Dr. Brian Weiss says it's possible to heal and grow your mind, body and soul, as well as strengthen your present-day relationships. He says one of the most common signs of a past life is déjà vu; the sensation that you have met a person before or have visited someplace previously. Sometimes, this déjà vu feeling could be a sign of a past life with a particular person or in a specific place.

During regression you still have an awareness of the present and some people watch their past as a movie while others feel, rather than see. Hypnotherapist, Alexandra Salkova McKenzie told me about Rachel who had come for a session because of claustrophobia. "Rachel regressed with ease and described herself as a 5 year old girl. Her family was moving from England to Sweden according to her observations, and it appeared to be in the early nineteen hundreds. Rachel's father was a businessman and they had led a very rich and comfortable life. As the story continued, Rachel found herself in a cabin on a ship. She could sense something was not right. The boat was sinking and she couldn't open the cabin door. In her mind, Rachel was kicking and screaming for the door to open and finally managed to open it. The next moment, she woke up on the shore. She had survived. Coming out of the trance state, Rachel confirmed the meaning of the story and felt relieved to understand her irrational fear and anxiety in confined spaces in this lifetime."

Life Between Lives

Taking explorations into past lives even further, hypnotherapist and counsellor Michael Newton found it was possible to see into the spirit world through the mind of a hypnotized subject who would not only report back on past lives, but a number would slip into the space between each lifetime. His fascinating book, *Journey of Souls*, is a series of case studies which reveal the mystery of life after death, expanding awareness of what is possible through hypnosis.

A Life Between Lives session is a deep hypnotic process that Newton developed over many years and designed in order to reconnect you with your soul, your soul group and your guides. It's an opportunity to understand the purpose for choosing this particular life incarnation.

Consider your soul as the 'I am' presence and your true identity that inhabits the vehicle you call your body. Without your soul you would just be a body, like a car without a driver, a light bulb without electricity or a computer with no software loaded. A soul is not just the driver of life; it also embodies the *why* of your very existence, meaning and purpose. At the end of your physical life, the soul resumes a spiritual state.

Your soul group is akin to a family whereby at times you hold hands and stay together while other times you drift apart to have different experiences. Yet your family remains your family whether you accept or reject them. And so it is with your soul group.

If you are in a drama with another person, a Life Between Lives experience might allow you to understand how you and the other person may have agreed, at the soul level, to play certain roles, and behave in certain ways in order to assist your development and growth.

A Life Between Lives session can be seen either as reality or a metaphor created by your mind to enable you to see a different perspective on life's challenges. It's as if you get an opportunity to peek behind the curtain that was placed when you chose to come into this lifetime and this time, space, reality and dimension. It's also useful to consider the main players in your life; the people you love or have loved or those who have made a strong impression and influenced you through your life. The Life Between Lives session can then enable you to understand the roles they agreed to play in order to create valuable learning experiences for you, and vice versa. Understanding the contracts you've made prior to coming into this lifetime often enables you to view particularly challenging situations and people from a new perspective, forgive them or thank them for the part they have played in your evolution and growth.

When I first met Joseph, he was going through a messy separation and divorce. Filled with anger and negativity, he believed that his wife had put a curse on him as the walls of his life appeared to collapse one by one. Because of this he began seeking help through alternative healing modalities, something that he would never have considered before. He began to notice that certain friends faded into the background of his life while others appeared opening the door to new possibilities. What if, at a soul level, Joseph and the soul that is playing the part of his wife, agreed to take on the roles to create a situation which would ultimately lead him to a better understanding of himself.

Just for a moment, consider the 'players' in your life. Who are the players who have been pivotal in some of the most impactful experiences of your life (positive and negative)? Now view the person and situation from a soul group perspective and you may begin to understand and bless the experience for where it has led or may be leading you today. When your life moves into a great space it becomes easier to see how the jigsaw pieces come together so beautifully!

My own Life Between Lives session started with a guided visualization which created a feeling of deep relaxation as I was gently regressed through childhood and into the womb. From there I immediately slipped into a lifetime several centuries ago appearing as a young female of poor means in my twenties. All was well and I was deeply in love with a young man. (I connected the young man to a powerful and deep relationship I had in this lifetime). Together, we had a child who died. Because I was inconsolable at the death of my child, the young man eventually left me. I was devastated. Fast forward a few more years in that regressed lifetime and I could feel my throat tighten. I was coughing and finding it challenging to breathe realizing the passing of that lifetime was near. Guided to move swiftly through the death scene and just 'let go,' there was an immediate relief and release. I felt myself soaring higher and higher and higher to be met by a 'guide.' And this is when I began an extraordinary journey to experience a Life Between Lives session.

I'm sure you too would love to know your life plan. Robert Schwartz brought the idea of pre-birth planning into play. Sharing stories in his books, *Your Soul's Plan* and *Your Soul's Gifts*, he interviewed people with a range of life challenges such as mental conditions, physical challenges and abusive relationships, allowing them to view the situation from a much higher perspective and gather the lessons their souls planned and came into this time, space and dimension to learn. Through these stories you too may develop a deeper insight into some of the people and situations you have attracted into your life.

If you believe that you are an eternal soul who has had many lives and many experiences then surely it would make sense that you would be able to access talents, gifts and experiences that you've had in other lives and be able to bring forth those gifts to use in the now. Surely, not everything you learn in each lifetime is wasted?

The Akash

Imagine the Akash (or Akashic Records as they are often called) as a complete library and history of all your thoughts, emotions, experiences and actions across all time and lifetimes; a place where simply *everything* is recorded. This library is not accessible by car, plane or ship. It can be accessed only through entering a different brain wave cycle.

So imagine being able to walk into a complete library to understand your purpose or why you have certain fears or aversions for no apparent reason. More than a personal library, the Akash is said to record everything that happens. Maybe you've felt the history of a particular place where, perhaps, a battle took place and you still feel the energy and fear that was present at that time.

In recent years there have been more and more documented cases of children recalling another lifetime. While many cultures accept that these memories can be brought through lifetimes, it is only recently that these cases have been researched and documented. In *Return to Life: Extraordinary Cases of Children Who Remember Past Lives,* a book published by psychiatry professor Jim Tucker, he investigates cases in which young children around the world shared recollections that seemed to be about someone else's life.

Just for a moment, consider that most ancient tribes and traditions always honor their ancestors, in reality they are honoring themselves. For in a past life you could have been your great, great, grandmother or grandfather and many healing modalities such as Family Constellations, sometimes known as Systemic Constellations, give you an opportunity to discover underlying family bonds and forces that have been carried unconsciously over several generations. This brings new meaning to when you heal and develop yourself here in the now; you are really healing up both past and future lifetimes.

You are far more than what you perceive yourself to be and once you start to recognize and awaken to this then you can begin to break free from the limits of your current reality.

When you make the connection to a deeper part of yourself and who you truly are, then you have access to guidance from a source that allows you to move forward moment by moment with grace and ease. After all, you are not limited by the glass ceiling above your head; it's actually the glass ceiling in your head!

Chapter Ten:

A Journey into the Indigenous World

"Imagine how your life would change if you lived in an open state of awareness where anything is possible!"

Carol Talbot

KEY QUESTIONS:

How do the indigenous tribes know what plants to use?

What has a giant green monkey tree frog got to do with your health?

How do the plants and indigenous medicines heal and help you?

"If you are coming to help us you are wasting your time. If you are coming because you know your liberation is bound up with ours, then let us work together." So say the Indigenous Tribal Elders.

The prophecy of the Eagle and the Condor

There is an ancient Amazon prophecy that speaks of a time when the Eagle and the Condor will come together. The Eagle and the Condor represent two different paths that highlight the huge split that is prevalent in our society. The Condor represents the feminine, the heart and intuition, while the Eagle symbolizes the path of the male, the mind, individualism and all that is scientific.

The prophecy predicts that during the first three cycles (of 500 years each), the Condor and the Eagle would fly separately, developing in their own way. In the fourth cycle, called pachakuchi, they would come together and clash in a way that the Eagle would nearly drive the Condor into extinction. This can be seen in the late 1400s with the Spanish discovering the Americas and the mass killing of the indigenous people, which still continues today as their land is sold for oil exploration and development.

During the fifth cycle which started around 2005, it is predicted that there is an opportunity, and the potential, for the Eagle and Condor to come together, and that the offspring of the Eagle and the Condor will bring a new consciousness; a time of understanding that there is plenty for all of us. Amen to that!

There is a huge misconception that indigenous people are uneducated and poor in many ways. Nothing could be farther from the truth. These people are not primitive or savage. Their wisdom comes from a deep connection with Mother Earth, a vast knowledge of the plant life around them and a deep respect for animals. In our so-called civilized world we have grown in terms of technology and our consumer lifestyle. It is called the knowledge age whereby we have the ability to connect with anyone in the world virtually instantly and quickly know what is going on anywhere around the globe. The real truth is that we have lost our connection to what is really important; our connection with this living breathing place we call home... Mother Earth.

The way to reconnect may be found in exploring nature and what grows from the earth itself.

Raising consciousness through plants

Two specific plants that many indigenous tribes in South America combine together form the sacred brew known as Ayahuasca or the 'vine of wisdom.' It is made from the stem of the ayahuasca vine (often referred to as 'the vine of the ancestors') and the leaves of the chacruna. In chemical terms, the leafy chacruna plant contains the powerful psychoactive dimethyltryptamine (DMT).

There are naturally occurring 'trace amounts' of DMT in the human body. When you are born and when you die, large amounts of DMT are naturally released into your system. If you drink the Ayahuasca plant brew, large amounts of DMT stream into your system which floods your pineal gland.

The pineal gland is located in the middle of the brain, and is often referred to as the 'third eye,' perhaps because of its connection to light or because it is at the same level as the eyes. Interestingly, the interior of the pineal gland has retinol tissue composed of rods and cones just like the eyes. It is even wired into the visual cortex of the brain.

French philosopher, René Descartes (he's the one who said, "I think, therefore I am"... in French of course!), was fascinated with the pineal gland and regarded it as the 'principal seat of the soul.' It produces melatonin, a hormone that affects the quality and duration of your sleep. It also regulates your daily and seasonal circadian rhythms. These are the sleep-wake patterns that determine your hormone levels, stress levels, and physical performance. So it may be a small gland, but it literally impacts how you think and feel every day!

You require both dark and light to activate and trigger your pineal gland in different ways. Any light stimulates the pineal gland to produce serotonin which is responsible for your mood and energy levels. Whereas darkness suppresses the production of serotonin and it then produces melatonin to ensure a good night's sleep. Hence sleeping with devices in a room such as a smartphone, laptop, and television etc. that have any light can disturb your sleep pattern.

As well as being associated with healing, Ayahuasca triggers powerful visionary experiences and can be used for shamanic journeys and to gain access to other realms that most people are unable to access in the normal waking state or solely through meditation.

My question was how did the indigenous tribes know to create this combination of two plants?

Many shamans will claim that the plants themselves taught them how to do this. And now, as Ayahuasca gains popularity (although it is illegal in many parts of the world) its resurgence can be seen as an aid to accelerate levels of consciousness as human beings and the planet evolve.

In Gabon and Cameroon, the Bwiti tribe use a perennial shrub and psychedelic known as Iboga. The iboga bark's visionary power is created by a mixture of alkaloids that seems to affect many of the known neurotransmitters, including serotonin and dopamine. The name of the plant is derived from 'Taber Ibo,' which literally means 'breaking open the head.' Iboga leads you into your unconscious mind and often gives insights into old patterns or habits to release and let go of, particularly addictions.

The experience can last several days. Starting with an opening ceremony on Friday evening, over the course of three days and two nights I experienced a gazillion images floating in and out and across my mind. Every time I peered closer to view an image it morphed into something else. I later concluded that my mind had experienced a massive cleanse and empty out, and I certainly felt the mind clutter had disappeared. One member of our group had been a heroin addict for over ten years. When our group reconvened on Sunday afternoon for sharing and a closing ceremony, she displayed none of the symptoms that would usually be associated with withdrawal for heavy duty drug addiction.

Ultimately, the indigenous plants have a way of taking you where you need to go more rapidly than might happen through meditation. Everyone's experience is different. You are often asked to keep specific questions in mind and with Iboga it is not the usual, 'what is my path?' or 'what was I put on earth to do?' questions, rather it is something more specific. The reason for this is that while you can ask about your path, there is so much more that can be shown, besides which it is hard to process the vast amount of information that would be available on all the possible paths of a lifetime.

Sharing his experience with me, Danny Saggars said, "the energy was powerful in my body and it felt as though the bottom half of my body was spiraling clockwise and the top half of my body was spiraling counter clockwise. I started seeing visions from my past and I was given clear answers concisely and easily, perhaps because Iboga is considered a masculine energy.

"I became a fish and felt how it was to swim through open water, I then experienced being in the body of a dog, a scorpion and some type of bird. It was a trip to feel the sensation of being in these different types of bodies with such different limbs and body composition. I saw how creation worked in terms of the oneness and connection between everything, and all life being given a divine spark of God; of pure love. I could understand how reincarnation happens with energies moving between vessels. As well as the past, I was given glimpses of the future and these were given as metaphors. And finally, a huge cinema screening area with red sash curtains was drawn back to reveal the word 'fear' in huge letters and relating to what's holding me back.

"Speaking to the facilitators afterwards, one of them called me 'Kuandoit.' When I asked the meaning he told me that it means 'spiral.'" The spiral or the never ending infinity whirlpool is a special reanimation energy that gifts you the power to reanimate the environment around you.

Of course, everyone's experience is different and I believe that the plants guide you to where you need to go and to see and feel what you need to see and feel. These ceremonies are part of the many shamanic traditions around the globe.

I mentioned shamanic traditions in an earlier chapter. It is one of the world's oldest healing traditions and holds the belief that *everything* is alive and carries with it power and wisdom. Power animals are often an essential component of shamanic practice in that each power animal that you have increases your power and lends you its wisdom. So for example, an owl has exceptional hearing so as a power animal, it can enable you to hear spirits or see through illusion. The monkey has messages of intelligence and intensity with a strong ability for compassion (I was delighted when it appeared as one of my power animals!).

It was high on a hillside in Peru, next to a small stream that I came to learn of the frog not only as a power animal but of its healing abilities. I was taking part in a Huachuma (sometimes referred to as San Pedro) ceremony which involved drinking a lumpy and decidedly disgusting substance from the cactus plant that made me heave and wretch. After drinking this lumpy juice, the plant first brings about drowsiness and a feeling of lethargy, followed by clearer vision and later, a sense of peace and tranquility. A perfect state to be in while outside in nature.

In this state I partnered with our group leader for a 'destiny session,' and for the first time heard about a powerful medicine called 'Kambo.' To be truthful with you, I felt no affinity with frogs and would have leapt up and screamed if one had jumped near me. Thinking no more of this session, it was years later that I found myself in a remote area of Portugal fainting and purging (along with an urgent need for the bathroom, if you get my drift) due to the powerful effects of a frog. This probably wins the award for the most intense training experience I've been through!

A bright green giant monkey tree frog has got a lot to do with your health! Kambo comes from a particular frog found in abundance in the Upper Amazon. It's a traditional medicine from the Amazon known by indigenous tribes to boost strength and stamina. Discovered to contain more than 200 bioactive peptides, it's now providing deep healing for people with a variety of conditions. It's powerful, and it works quickly as a mental, physical and emotional healer.

As a symbol, the frog teaches us how to jump from one level to another; perhaps from materialism to spirituality. As a power animal, the frog can help you acclimatize to a new life, after all, as an adult it emerges from water to land. The frog is also associated with replenishment, cleansing and nurturing of the self. And this is what I learned for myself. This is the space I hold as I guide others through a powerful Kambo ceremony.

Julya said, "I felt the Kambo move through my system almost immediately and the next 10, 15, 20, 25 minutes (time disappeared) were truly intense for me." Racing around the lymph system, Kambo gathers all the toxins in the body into the gut ready for purging (one way or another). "My head and face felt swollen and my heart was pounding, yet despite this temporary discomfort I was aware that every part of my being and body was being scanned. I even felt my right kidney speaking to me asking for attention."

The indigenous tribes use Kambo to fight 'panema,' which means sadness, lack of luck, irritation and bad energy. "I didn't think I had any sadness in me but Kambo knew better. As I purged I felt all the sadness leaving my space and gathering in the bucket before me."

Julya's story does not end there. She told me that later the same day "I connected to all the sadness around me, particularly the headlines about the Syrian refugees. I connected to every child, brother, sister, mother, and father. To the oppressors and the victims, to the wounds and fears and feelings of hopelessness; I connected to people in my life as well as parts of myself. The things I did and didn't do, what I said or did not say, what I thought and felt. And I cried. I wept it all out until after some time, it transformed into compassion and as it did, I felt a major reset happening within me. And I smiled. I had gone for a Kambo session to detox my physical body and ultimately healed my heart."

The only thing you have to fear is fear itself. The emotion of fear, rather than the reality of what you fear is what causes you anxiety, stress and unhappiness. When you touch what you fear it simply disappears.

Follow the signs!

Spirals

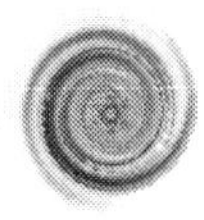

Different information is available at different brain wave cycles and one of the optimum states for learning is Alpha. It is hard-wired to the parasympathetic nervous system which means it is impossible to feel a negative emotion when you are operating from this brain wave cycle. It allows you to access the 'power of now.'

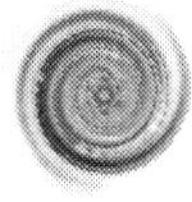

Scientists have discovered that Theta brain frequency can alleviate stress, reduce anxiety, facilitate deep relaxation, improve mental clarity and creative thinking, reduce pain, promote euphoria, and provide access to instant healings. Withdrawing from the external world, many people cite mystical experiences while in this slow brain rhythm.

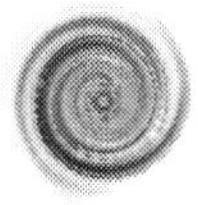

Hypnosis works by partially suspending the constant self-chatter that you may have experienced when meditating, allowing more direct communication with your unconscious mind and allowing you to tap into the wisdom within. It's the key that unlocks the door into your thoughts, memories, emotions and so much more that is stored at the unconscious level of the mind.

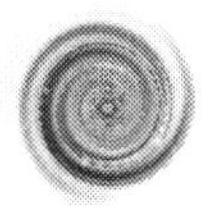

Trance states allow you to connect with your very own wisdom within. As well as accessing past lives, you can utilize trance states to link in to the life between lives thus gaining a deeper understanding of your life purpose as well as the agreements you made with other souls. There is a huge library – a complete history of all your thoughts, emotions and actions across all time and lifetimes - available to tap into.

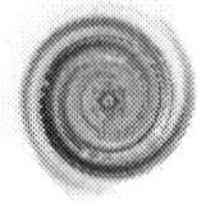

The Eagle and the Condor represent two different paths that highlight the huge split that is prevalent in our society. An ancient indigenous prophecy predicts that there is an opportunity, and the potential, for the Eagle and Condor to come together, and that the offspring of the Eagle and the Condor will bring a new consciousness, a time of understanding that there is plenty for all of us.
The time is NOW.

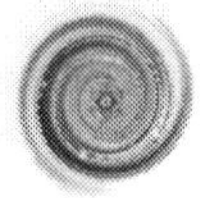

Many of the indigenous tribes of the world gift us with an opportunity to understand and connect with Mother Earth to gain a deeper insight and wisdom. Their knowledge and experience with plant and animal medicines bring visions and insights to accelerate and raise consciousness rapidly.

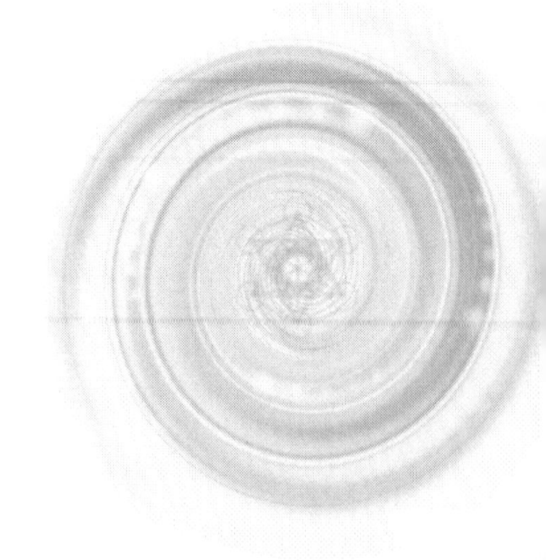

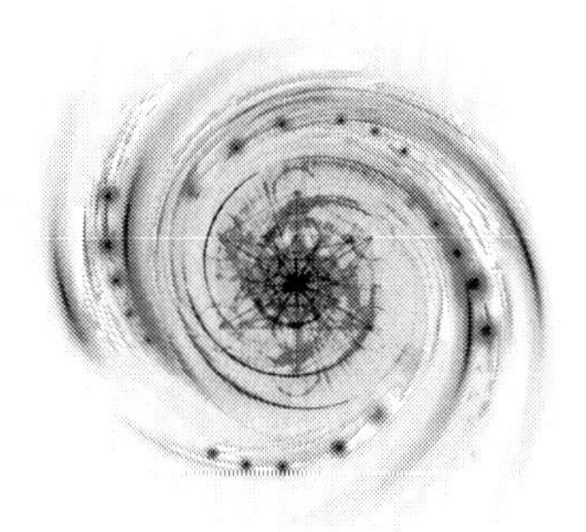

Part Four:

A NEW YOU-NIVERSE

"To know thyself will set you free."

Socrates

The most profound experiences of your life are always going to be 'beyond words,' and the plants of the indigenous tribes offer powerful experiences to reconnect to who you truly are and to experience the bigger picture.

After a day of cleansing and fasting, we had been led into the rainforest by our guide and after several hours, we stepped out of the rainforest into the clearing that was home to a small Achuar community. Located on a ridge looking down on the Pastaza River, I could not have imagined a more perfect setting for my first experience with the spirit vine. To date, I still view this setting as one of the most beautiful places I've ever been and part of that was maybe the energy that I felt in that place.

As the sun set, a small group of us took turns drinking a full cup of the brew and then made our way to lay back on huge banana leaves and gaze up at the clear, unpolluted sky lit up with a billion stars.

It may have been forty minutes later, or perhaps only five minutes, for time ceases and has little relevance, when I felt a light spray of sparkles shower me from head to toe as I 'tripped' back to a psychedelic era of beautiful colors, shapes and cartoons. Yes! Cartoons! Not what I was expecting from a supposedly spiritual experience! And then I simply died. I drowned and it felt like the right thing to do.

Of course, I didn't actually drown or die, yet perhaps a part of me did.

As I lay back on a banana leaf, and I'm not sure whether my eyes were open or closed, hovering above me was a huge spaceship. When I say 'huge,' it covered the whole sky. As it hovered high in the sky, I felt as if it were scanning every part of me, until I looked up and saw that the spaceship was me! I was looking down on my very self.

The spacecraft appeared to be a specific geometrical shape that I later came to learn, and after much searching, was known as the Vector Equilibrium. According to Synergetics by Hermann Haken, 'the Vector Equilibrium is the zero starting point for happenings or non-happenings; it is the empty theater, the empty circus and empty universe ready to accommodate any act or any audience.' Wow, what a profound message. Years later, that moment in time still continues to create more insights, highlighting the ripple effect and impact of experiences.

Our guides had encouraged us to keep some questions in mind throughout the experience, and I had plenty! I must have asked hundreds of questions and within seconds would receive the answer; admittedly not always the answer I expected or would have liked.

And then the purging began... and continued, and continued, and continued (akin to your worst drinking nightmare). Please note that not everyone purges but it seems to be common with me! So there I was, lying crumpled on a banana leaf in the heart and lungs of the world with the sound of Sumpa, our shaman, whistling and rustling feathers, his sound and song fading in and out as he guided me to a deeper truth that resided within me. And it had been there all along.

The following morning, I met with our Achuar shaman who was very happy with my experience with the sacred vine. And so he should be as he had guided my journey and removed the blocks and fears that had held me back. In fact he said I had journeyed like an Achuar tribal woman. The moment he said those words, tears welled up in my eyes. Tears of joy!

And then I was left with a big 'what does it all mean?' and 'what do I do after one of the most powerful experiences of my life?' And so another quest began, like the shapes within a vast jigsaw puzzle starting to come together.

Chapter Eleven:

Follow the Signs

"Everyone and everything in the universe is interconnected. Stay pure of heart and you will see the signs. Follow the signs and you will uncover your destiny."

From the movie, 'Jeff Who Lives At Home.'

KEY QUESTIONS:

What is Sacred Geometry and is it important?

How does Sacred Geometry relate to you?

What is the 'shape' of things to come?

I was flicking channels on a long haul flight when the quote above made me pause and watch an entire movie I had never heard of before. In summary, Jeff is a 30 something, unemployed young man living in his mother's basement while he looks for signs about his purpose and what to do with his life. He answers a telephone call that turns out to be a wrong number asking for 'Kevin.' Leaving the basement on an errand for his mother he sees someone on the bus wearing a t-shirt with the name 'Kevin,' and so on a whim, he follows him. This leads him into a series of mishaps and experiences interwoven with his mother, brother and sister-in-law, which finally leads him to his destiny.

You too are linked and interwoven with everyone and everything in your life.

By following the signs that I had seen above me in the skies of Ecuador with the Achuar tribe, I found myself linked and interwoven with a group of travelers high in the Andes mountains in Peru, at the Incan citadel that is known as Machu Picchu. Eavesdropping on a conversation halfway up Wayna Picchu, I heard the name 'Drunvalo Melchizedek.' "Unusual name," I thought, and made a mental note to research the name on Google. A few weeks later I was totally immersed in two of Drunvalo Melchizedeks' books, *The Flower of Life Volumes 1 and 2.*

What is the Flower of Life? It's the modern name given to a geometrical figure composed of multiple evenly-spaced, overlapping circles that are arranged so that they form a flower-like pattern with a six-fold symmetry like a hexagon.

Flower of Life

When I look at this beautiful pattern it reminds me of one of my favorite pastimes as a child, which was using 'Spirograph.' It's a mathematical toy, although I was unaware of that at the time as I placed a colored pen through one of the holes of a small rolling circle within a fixed circle. When you roll it inside the bigger fixed circle you create wonderful circular designs that have a mesmerizing effect.

From a New Age perspective the Flower of Life offers a deep spiritual meaning and forms of enlightenment to those who have studied it as part of Sacred Geometry. It is said to contain the patterns of creation and encode the structures of our reality. Not only that, this symbol can be found in all major religions, and in many areas of the world from The Temple of Osiris in Abydos, Egypt, to The Forbidden City in Beijing, China, and many other places around the globe.

I felt this was profound, for it meant that what I had seen in the skies of Ecuador was not simply random shapes that appeared to be spacecraft. The signpost was clearly pointing me in the direction of shapes and Sacred Geometry.

Sacred Geometry is the basic fundamental building block of our universe based on mathematics and form. It is found in all of nature whether that is in spirals, hexagonal structures or pentagonal shapes, the platonic solid structures, crystal structures, the tube torus, stones, and more.

Johannes Kepler said, "Where there is matter, there is geometry," and you are matter! You are created from the very simplest (yet complex) of things; a single cell that has been fertilized. And the possibilities are quite spectacular. While the single celled amoebas that you learned about in Chapter 4 simply divide and become more amoebas, the first human fertilized cell (or egg) splits into 2, then 4, then 8, 16, 32, 64, 128 and so on. It is beginning a journey that over the next nine months produces descendant cells with different shapes and functions (neurons, red and white blood cells, cells of the ears, eyes, skin, etc.). You are created from the simple cell to become a human being of enormous complexity, shape and potential and Sacred Geometry gives you a visual representation of moving from the simple to the complex.

So let's start at the beginning and imagine a single point, or dot of consciousness that gets curious and expands in all directions. If that point of consciousness expands outwards from the single point or dot in all directions, draw a line around it and you will get a circle. You may want to grab a pen and draw this out. Ever more curious, the point of consciousness expands further by moving to the edge of the circle (anywhere) and repeats itself, which creates two circles that overlap each other. The place where they overlap is called the Vesica Piscis which contains geometric information about light.

For light to exist there must be dark, for you live in a world of duality. However, light and dark are not simply polar opposites. You cannot shine dark into a light area and the whole area goes dark. Yet when you shine light into a dark area, it lightens the whole area.

As Rudolph Steiner said, "Light cannot reveal itself alone and on its own; shadows or darkness must be present as well, therefore, you have a duality. The Good could never reveal itself if Evil were not there as its shadow-picture. The duality of Good and Evil is an essential in the manifested world."

What this means is for you to be truly whole and complete you must embrace all aspects of yourself, the light and dark.

You might also notice that the Vesica Piscis is the shape of the eye, and it is through the eyes that we perceive the world and can view light and the reflection of the creation of our thoughts, emotions, language and beliefs.

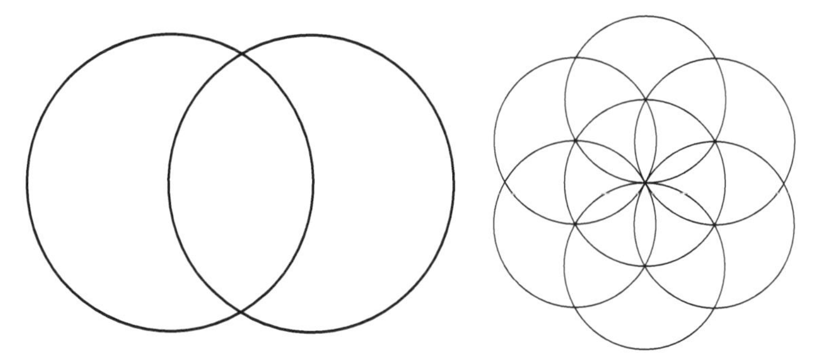

Vesica Piscis and Seed of Life

From the two overlapping circles of the Vesica Piscis, the pattern expands further to create the Seed of Life (also referred to as the Genesis pattern). Every civilization has the Seed of Life pattern within their art which highlights humanity's connection. The Seed of Life creates the tube Torus (which looks like a donut) and shows how energy moves in its most balanced dynamic flow process. Actually, the human heart with its seven muscles forms a Torus and this 'energy field' is around all life forms, all atoms, and all cosmic bodies such as planets, stars and galaxies. Researcher Arthur Young said, *"The self in a toroidal Universe can be both separate and connected with everything else."*

The Seed of Life expands and evolves to create the Flower of Life, which contains the Tree of Life, a structure that dates back 3,000 years ago in ancient Egypt, as well as being at the heart of the sacred teachings of the Jewish Kabbalah.

If you observe the beauty and possibilities in this evolution and expansion perhaps you are beginning to understand the possibilities that lie within your own evolution and expansion.

The Flower of Life is usually shown with a boundary around it. No doubt you have placed boundaries and limitations around yourself about what is possible or not. Where in your life do you say 'that's impossible,' or 'I could never do that,' or 'I'm afraid?' Remember, there are only two fears encoded in the human DNA; the fear of falling and the fear of loud noises. Any other fears whether that is snakes, dogs, flying, change, relationships, public speaking, failure, not being good enough, whatever it may be, are fears that you have acquired throughout your life.

Anaïs Nin said, "And the day came when the risk to remain tight in a bud was more painful than the risk it took to blossom." The Flower of Life blossoms when you remove the outer boundary. If you continue the circles that were cut off by the outer circle and boundary and add the missing circles, it becomes the Fruit of Life which is viewed by many to be the blueprint of the universe.

What would happen if you removed the boundaries of who you believe yourself to be and expanded your mind? As Ralph Waldo Emerson said, "the mind, once stretched by a new idea, never returns to its original dimensions."

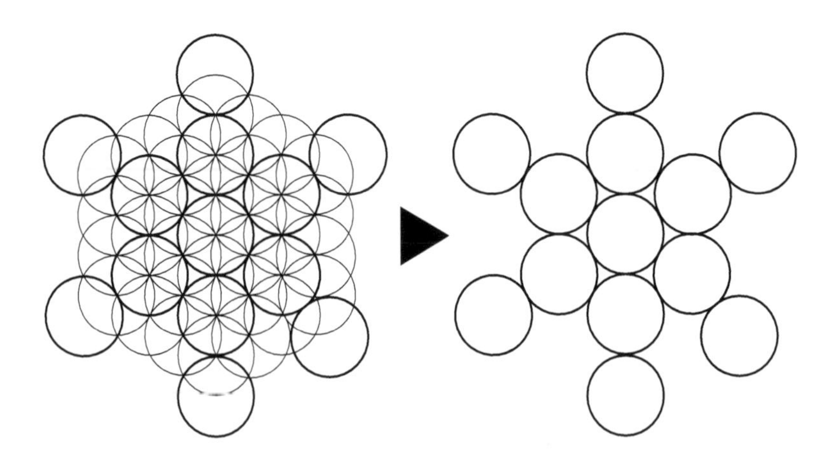

Fruit of Life from Flower of Life

Now stay with me on this... and allow me to stretch your mind a little further. Up until now, you have seen curved lines and circular shapes. Feminine energy is associated with curved lines while straight lines are associated with masculine energy. Something spectacular is created when you add straight lines.

When you draw a line from the center of each circle to every other circle, what you will get is referred to as Metatron's Cube. While the image below is two dimensional, when you view this as three dimensional you'll understand the movement that is also inherent in the pattern.

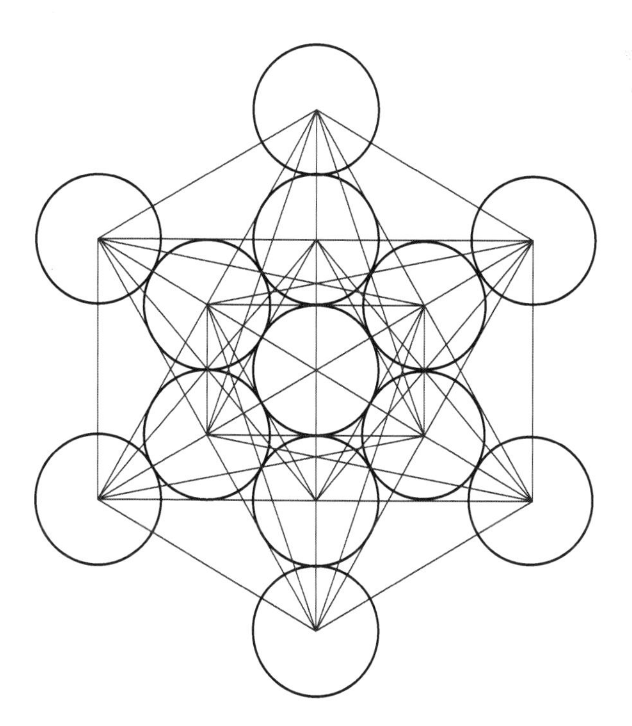

Metatron's Cube

Metatron's Cube is known as one of the most important informational systems in our universe. Metatron is the holder of the keys to the

Universe and all that resides within it. Everything that exists in this space, time, reality and dimension does so because of Sacred Geometry. Nothing would exist without it. YOU are the key to your universe when you choose to embrace ALL of you; masculine, feminine, dark and light.

Within Metatron's Cube, the lines and intersecting points create five unique shapes known as the platonic solids. Each of these shapes can fit inside a sphere with all corners touching the edge of the sphere.

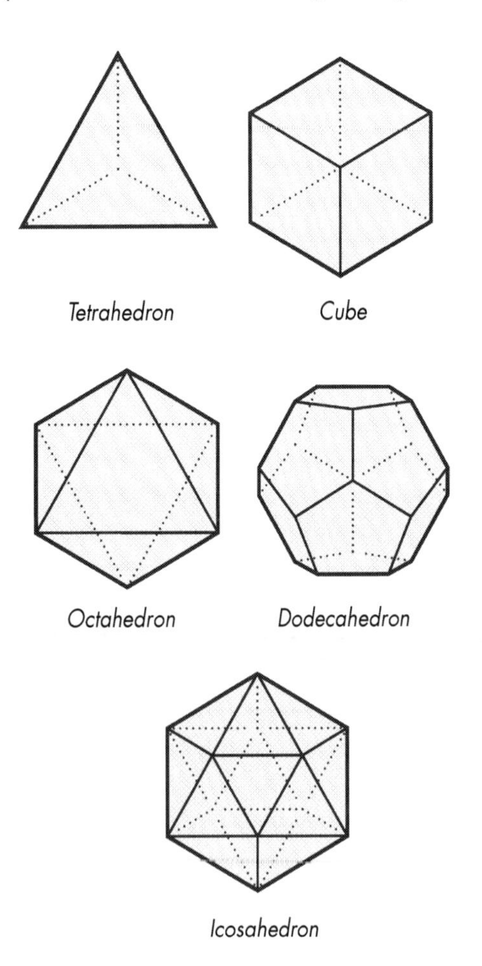

Nice shapes and patterns, you may be thinking! So what? How does it relate to you, and why is it called **Sacred Geometry?**

When you are just relating to the shapes it is simply geometry. However, when you begin to connect the shapes to consciousness, you're creating Sacred Geometry. As you notice the circles and shapes forming and interacting with each other it can give you an insight into your own evolution and the divine nature held within every cell of your body as each of your cells interact together as a community. **You can begin to notice that *everything* is built on shapes and patterns including yourself and the life you have created for yourself.**

You can either remain static in your life, confined by the shape, boundaries, fears, patterns and beliefs you have placed around yourself or, as more information becomes available, you can expand your awareness.

You and your body are an expression of your language, thoughts, feelings, emotions, experiences, memories, awareness and consciousness, and just as the geometric shapes evolve, expand and stand separately, they also come together in the most exquisite ways. And you do too. In life, you grow, learn, evolve, expand, stand separately yet also interact with everything and everyone around you. There's a connection. You are reflected into the world and the world is reflected in you.

There is another mystical shape also found within Metatron's Cube that I want to bring to your attention. It's the star tetrahedron, made up of two tetrahedrons. It is also referred to as the Merkaba or Mer-ka-ba. In ancient Egyptian, 'mer' means rotating fields of light, 'ka' means spirit and 'ba' refers to the soul.

Star Tetrahedron/Merkaba

Therefore, Mer-ka-ba means the spirit or energy body surrounded by counter-rotating fields of light, or spirals of energy which transport spirit or consciousness from one dimension to another. When the two tetrahedrons are spinning in opposite directions, it becomes the spinning Light Body vehicle supposedly used by Ascended Masters to connect with and tune into higher realms and enables you to connect with the Divine. In order to do that, there needs to be alignment.

Your Merkaba is your very own super-turbo-charged sports car, but like any car, if it has a flat tire, while you can still drive, it will likely be a bumpy ride. So with practice, using the energy and shape visualization of a Merkaba, you can activate an energy field around you which is capable of carrying your consciousness directly to higher realms and expanding your awareness.

While consciousness could be described as being aware of your surroundings and your physical body, what I mean by consciousness is becoming aware of your spiritual nature and being more than just a physical body. You are more than your language, thoughts, memories, beliefs, emotions, patterns and physical body. In fact, you have a mental body, physical body and emotional body emanating from spirit. The magic happens when you align and engage the mental, physical and emotional bodies. For example, when you get clear about an outcome or goal you are activating your mental body using intellect and logic. It is only when you merge your goal and outcome with physically acting as if you are achieving that outcome and engaging your emotions does the universe truly respond. For example, the indigenous tribes never pray 'for rain,' because that would presuppose that it has not rained yet. They simply pray 'rain!' If you watch any of the videos of the 'no medicine' hospitals in China, they are not chanting for healing to take place. They chant 'it's done.' And it is.

Another example would be when illness and dis-ease manifests in the physical body. It is the physical body that allopathic medicine addresses. Only when the thought patterns (mental body) and emotions (emotional body) are also addressed can true healing take place.

Our world is based on interacting shapes, and the patterns in Sacred Geometry allow you to fully consider your creative abilities as the shapes intertwine, expand inwards and outwards from the simple to the complex as you connect your physical, mental and emotional bodies.

There is much more to Sacred Geometry that I encourage you to explore for it also reflects the fractal and holographic nature of how we perceive the world. A fractal, a term coined by Benoit B.

Mandlebrot, is a never-ending pattern that repeats. **What patterns are you choosing to repeat and recreate in your life?**

Throughout history, numerous clues and hints regarding geometry, sound, frequency and vibration have been seemingly waiting, like a giant puzzle, for the pieces to be put together. Harmony is the key and Sacred Geometry is created through sound. The shape of you and your universe is literally brought forth into being through sound.

Chapter Twelve:

Good Vibrations!

"You are matter, therefore
YOU MATTER!"

Carol Talbot

KEY QUESTIONS:

Why is sound and frequency important?

What does it mean to be 'vibrationally aligned?'

How do you get into vibrational alignment?

San Miguel de Allende in central Mexico has recently been listed as a UNESCO World Heritage Site. Some locals believe that the town was built on a bed of quartz crystals, amplifying its rejuvenating nature so it is easy to understand why visitors fall in love with this magical city. I certainly did.

Gloria Belendez Ramirez is a true ambassador for happiness and a dear friend. Villas Xichu is the retreat center she created and built with love and care in San Miguel de Allende. It became my home for several glorious weeks as I explored more along a shamanic path and deeper journey into my heart with Paloma Blanca. The world of sound was about to be opened up to me.

My guide on this journey, Christina Sol, carries an unusual category of Ayahuasca which she calls Paloma Blanca. It is often referred to as Ayahuasca of the Moon, the White Dove, the White Deer and Medicine of the Sacred Heart. Christina believes that perception changes when you practice observing the world through the eye of your heart.

The experience requires at least three separate sessions during which sound and music plays, allowing for the opening of your energetic system so that a high vibration of your soul can merge into your physical body.

During all three of my sessions I kept hearing what I can only describe as the 'sound beyond the sound.' Lying perfectly still, I knew it wasn't a part of the music being played through the physical speakers because the sound was so different, yet it also blended perfectly.

You are energy

Sound can be defined as vibrational energy and according to science, everything in our universe is made up of energy vibrating at specific frequencies. Energy is everywhere, and is the building block of all matter. You and your body are composed of the same energy that also makes the chair that you're sitting on, the home that you live in, animals, trees and so on. It's all energy that is constantly flowing and changing form all the time.

Your energy can be referred to as your life force. In the Indian culture, energy is referred to as Prana, in traditional Chinese culture, it's called Qi (pronounced 'key'). In *Star Wars* it was referred to as 'The Force!' So may 'the force' be with you!

Imagine your energy as a field in you and around you. If your energy is low then your energy field is like thick mist or fog so you cannot see where you are going, and you cannot be seen. It's as if you're invisible. Several days after a cleansing ceremony, Charlotte told me she was at a party and it was as if she had suddenly become visible. People she had known of for ages seemed drawn to her.

Burning herbs to cleanse the energy around a person or space is common in many cultures around the world. In the Middle East it's often with frankincense, in India incense sticks and cones are used, South American tribes use palo santo (sacred wood) while the Native Americans use sage. Using any of these is a quick and gentle way to cleanse your own energy field.

You may have come across Master Zhou on television programs such as *Ripley's Believe It Or Not*, and *That's Incredible.* Master Zhou is a Qi Gong, Tai Chi and Kung Fu Grand Master and Master Medical Qi Gong Healer. Using energy alone, he is able to raise the temperature of water to boiling point with his hands, dry mud with his hands and set fire to paper simply with the energy emanating from his hands. He can also stand on thin sheets of paper without falling through them. A powerful demonstration of the energy available to you! What Master Zhou is doing is focusing the energy to create a condensed pool of energy allowing him to create all sorts of amazing feats.

You too, have vast amounts of energy available to you and what I've noticed is that many people have become desensitized to feeling and connecting with energy. It doesn't mean it isn't there. So let me share an exercise I learned in Qi Gong which can be used to release physical, mental and emotional stress as well as an awareness technique for 'feeling energy' or Qi in your body. You literally bounce and shake, loosening all your joints and release energy blockages from your mind and body.

Wherever you are right now (perhaps wait a while if you're in the middle of a coffee shop) stand up for a moment and start the movement from your feet, just bouncing up and down on your toes and heels... and be gentle. Continue while you also begin to shake out your hands and arms and just shake and bounce your whole body in an up and down motion for about one to two minutes. Then simply be still as you continue to feel the energy and internal vibrations racing in and around your body. It's very powerful, as well as energizing, and clearly demonstrates that you are energy, constantly vibrating.

An even easier exercise is to simply rub your hands together vigorously for at least a minute and then hold your hands about six to twelve inches apart and feel the energy you have generated flowing between your two hands.

So you, as a human being, are simply pure energy. You are energy and everything around you is energy and that means you are entangled and *connected to everything around you*. How you behave, how you think and feel is also vibrating into this field of energy. Your vibration and positive energy can and does affect and impact others.

You have no doubt been taught to listen to your thoughts and logic rather than go with the vibrations that you feel. Yet I'm sure you have experienced being around certain people who seem to sap every last drop of energy from you. You feel exhausted just being near them. Then there are others who raise your energy and it feels good to be in their presence.

Our planet and everything on it is energy that is vibrating. Your thoughts are vibrating. Your feelings and your desires are vibrating. All of your sense organs are reading vibrations and translating them into different forms of information such as light, sound, taste, touch and smell.

When you want something or set an intention or desire through your mind or verbally out loud through your language, words and feelings, a vibration is being emitted into the universe and this is what the Law of Attraction responds to. The Law of Attraction states that 'like attracts like,' so whether you are aware of it or not, you are responsible for the good, the bad and the ugly influences in your life.

For the human brain words have a meaning and a sound. Your brain associates with the words, as well as the sound and intention, emotion and intensity. I remember being surprised when one of my clients displayed a huge tattoo on his arm with the words 'on the edge.' He explained that another symbol tattooed on his wrist meant 'on-off.' He sees the symbol and those words on a regular basis, and those words transfer to his brain. It was no surprise to me that his challenge was to do with an addiction. He was literally 'on the edge!'

Using the right words and sounds is the way to communicate with your mind. In fact, a specific tone and words can be used to release pain. Perhaps you can remember your parents using a soothing voice to calm you down when you fell over or hurt yourself.

When you hear sound, you are *hearing* energy. When you are creating sounds (which can also be through your words and language) you are transmitting energy.

For eons, mystics have been telling us that it is sound that creates matter and form. In the *Bible* it is written "In the beginning was the Word." The Aborigines, who have walked the earth for over 40,000 years say that the world was sung into existence. Mystics believe the world is a reflection of infinite combinations of sound patterns. Sound affects how matter itself vibrates and can change how matter vibrates. That would mean that it can affect how YOU vibrate.

Good vibrations

Vibration and frequency go together. Everything vibrates at different frequencies, including you. To understand vibration, put your lips lightly together and let out the sound 'mmmmmm.' If you do this a few times you will feel your lips vibrate and a tingling feeling. This is a physical feeling of vibration.

The frequency is the rate of vibration and tells you how high or low the sound is. A low pitch equals a low frequency and a high pitch equals a high frequency.

I have a beautiful gong, and when I strike it with a mallet it moves back and forth creating this softer and louder effect that is very hypnotic and soothing. This also highlights the physical effect of sound on you depending on the source of the sound and if the sound is moving towards you or away from you.

All matter is governed by sound frequencies. You are matter. That means you are governed by sound frequencies and carry a certain frequency.

Every structure on earth, including you, has a particular frequency, a natural frequency at which it will vibrate. Sound waves are physical vibrations which can be tuned to physical structures. You've probably heard of the crystal glass that shatters when an opera singer hits a particular pitch and frequency. The frequency vibrates the glass and so it breaks.

Dr. Jeffrey Thompson, a chiropractor, began experimenting with sound and its effects on the body. What he discovered was that each part of the spine has a specific frequency that it resonates at, unique to each individual. Using the exact sound frequencies of the specific part of the spine, he made chiropractic spinal and cranial adjustments, to stimulate and normalize organ function, and to balance acupuncture meridians. Clinical research with patients and volunteers led him to identify the level that was out of balance to the point where he could simply play a note on a keyboard and the vertebra would shake itself back into alignment.

All parts of your body vibrate. A healthy body has a frequency between 62 – 72 (M)Hz. When your frequency drops, your immune system is compromised. Just for a moment consider that your body and your cells have their own song and when you tune into that, you can experience a profound balancing and alignment. This is what sound healers do. They direct frequencies into the body to restore harmony.

Your life is in harmony with the vibration and frequency you are sending out.

It is your frequency that places you in this specific time, space and dimension of what you perceive as reality. Your frequency is like your fingerprint. Your frequency is different from other things in the universe which gives you the illusion of being separate from what you perceive around you.

Take a moment to consider what is manifesting in your life right now in the areas of abundance, love, relationships, career, finances, health, friendships, family etc. You are in harmony with what is in your life right now.

Let me explain to you how that works through the analogy of a guitar. If you pluck one of the strings on a guitar, and there is a second guitar next to it, then the same string on the second guitar will start vibrating to align with the string that was plucked on the first guitar. The first guitar affects the second guitar. If you stop the sound of the string vibrating on the first guitar, for example by placing your hand across it, does the second guitar also stop vibrating? No, because if you then remove your hand from the strings on the first guitar, the second guitar will now affect the first guitar. It's a two way street. **What you send out into the world bounces right back at you** whether that be love, or lack of love, abundance, or lack of abundance, vitality or lack of vitality.

The field of cymatics offers you an opportunity to see a visual representation of how sound impacts you and your world. Cymatics is the science of sound made visible. It is based on the principle that when sound encounters a membrane such as your skin or the surface of water, it imprints an invisible pattern of energy. Taking water or sand placed on a membrane (which could be stretched plastic on a plate), a tone is made and what you will see as the sounds are played are beautiful geometries depending upon the pitch, tone, amplitude and modulation. You will see shapes that link back to Sacred Geometry!

A popular sound to chant is 'Om,' a powerful word in Sanskrit. When 'Om' is played in a cymatic type system it creates a complex pattern (nine interlocking triangles that surround and radiate from a central point) called the Sri Yantra, also known as the Cosmic Yantra. Again, this highlights the connection of Sacred Geometry and Sonic Geometry and how sound creates shapes.

I often put water into one of my Tibetan sound bowls, as a visual demonstration of the power of sound. As I move the stick around the perimeter of the sound bowl it vibrates and the water literally begins to dance.

Dr. Masaru Emoto, a Japanese researcher, provided factual evidence that our thoughts, ideas, emotions, words and voice affect human energy and vibration. In some of his experiments, he used words such as 'thank you' and 'you disgust me' and simply said them to water or stuck labels on bottles of water with specific words. Later, when tested, the water labelled with 'thank you' formed stunning symmetrical water crystals while the water labelled with 'you disgust me' formed unsymmetrical and ugly water crystals. Interestingly, experiments with classical music played to the water produced symmetrical crystals while heavy metal produced the opposite.

Thank You

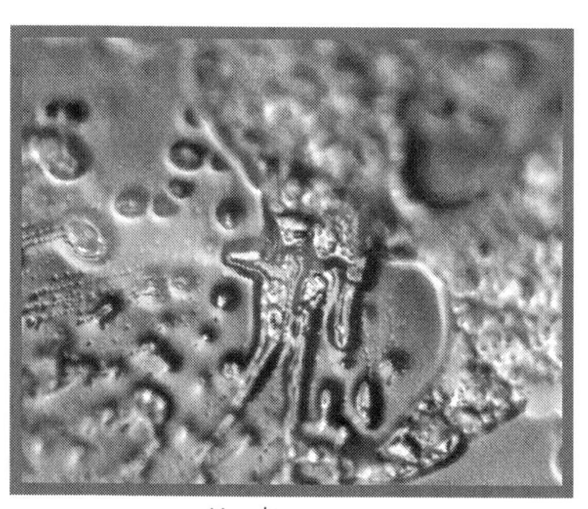

You disgust me

(Images used with permission from Office Masaru Emoto LLC)

A large amount of your body is made up of water so with every word you say, every sound you make, every thought you think, every emotion that you feel you are impacting your energy, vibration and frequency in some way, thereby impacting what you are creating and manifesting in your world.

The power of your voice

With your own voice, you can actually make two sounds or more at the same time and this is called over-toning. Overtone chanting is said to have originated in Mongolia where this is the 'normal' way of singing. In Tibet, the monks chant to connect with the Divine and throughout the world of shamans and spiritual leaders this form of over-toning has been used to enter the spirit world. Chanting this way creates a very beautiful vibrational effect throughout your nervous system, balancing and relaxing the whole body.

Another form of chanting uses a pattern called an open fifth which is a pair of notes where one frequency is 50% higher than another frequency. Esoterically, this particularly pattern of sound was said to open portals to different dimensions. In fact, it is said that when the monks were chanting these particularly sounds, they could manifest physical objects. Miraculous healings would occur and it was as if the sounds could actually speak to our DNA.

At an angel healing circle with Zoe Henderson, a gifted psychic and healer, we spent time chanting Eee Nu Rah Zay. Each sound has a meaning which, put together, creates the mantra, "I bring all of myself, mind, body, soul, emotions together in the company of angels." It is an easy way to say, "Angels I am here and ready to be with you." During the course of the evening we must have chanted this sound over 150 times and as we left, Zoe informed us that during the next day we would find a white feather to indicate that our request to the angels had been heard and they were working on it! To be honest, I thought nothing more of it, yet lo and behold, at various times during the following day I found three white feathers which I keep in a jar to remind me of the ability to manifest through sound.

The secret to creation

Sound, vibration and frequency are the very essence of creation. Listen to the rhythm of your heart, the sound of leaves rustling in trees, the sound of a bubbling stream. Sound holds a powerful key to understanding your life.

You are energy vibrating at a specific frequency. Remember that your thoughts, language and emotions are all vibrating at a specific frequency, creating energy and giving shape and patterns to your life. What you choose to create in your world comes from your energy vibrating at a specific frequency and you can shift your energy, vibration and frequency through sound and the words that you use to create a different pattern and shape to your life. As the great genius, Nikola Tesla said, "If you want to find the secrets of the universe, think in terms of energy, frequency, and vibration." And start singing!

Chapter Thirteen:

A New Perspective

"You are always more than you think you are."

Anon

KEY QUESTIONS:

What creates a vibrational shift?

How do you create a transformation?

How do you impact others?

I was in the USA attending a series of conferences which included a five day women's experience in Dallas. On the second evening, I was enjoying some of the impromptu sessions in the exhibition area, sipping champagne accompanied with chocolate covered strawberries. Catherine, one of the few people I knew at the event, rushed over and said, "there's someone who wants to meet you." I turned around and our eyes instantly locked in a way that communicates 'I know you.' He looked at the shapes that I was constantly drawing and doodling and declared, "you're from Antares." At that time, I had no idea whether Antares was a tropical island paradise in the Caribbean or another planetary system. It turned out to be the latter and as weird as that may sound; it felt very right and true for me.

David Gross is a teacher and a modern day monk at the core of his being. A third generation psychic medium, his gifts of insight have been refined through years of travel in Asia and time spent with revered teachers from Tibet, Japan, Vietnam, China and Thailand. To me he is simply my soul brother and answered a deeper calling for a connection to other like-minded souls. It felt as if the universe had not only masterminded our meeting, but gifted me an opportunity to receive information from a different dimension.

There is a lot of talk about shifting to a different 'dimension,' for example from our three dimensional reality to a fourth, fifth or to even higher dimensions. You already now know that you and everything around you is energy, vibration and frequency, so consider different dimensions as levels of density. In the third dimension, 'reality' is experienced as dense, heavy and solid. Time is understood as linear, meaning the belief is that the past creates the present and the future. That means that when you set a goal and get clear and specific about what you want, you then create a step by step plan to achieve the goal. Let's suppose you have set yourself a goal to generate a specific income over the next six months. In the linear model, that means you would set targets for yourself each month to achieve. If the first month does not go as well as expected and you fall short of the monthly target, you would double your target for the second month to make up for the shortfall. While you pick up the pace on the second month with more calls and meetings, you still fall short of your target, which means month three has an even higher target. It's also likely that your motivation begins to dwindle and the hope of reaching your six month goal begins to fade. Does this sound familiar?

As you raise your awareness and expand your understanding that you and everything around you is energy, vibration and frequency, feelings such as anger, hate or being a victim start to disappear and you literally 'feel lighter.' This is living in the now and the power of being present in the now. The past no longer needs to impact your present in a negative way. And as you start to open up to the idea that time is non-linear, you also open up to new possibilities. The non-linear approach means completely trusting your unconscious mind, getting into vibrational alignment, which may mean certain action needs to be taken, and allowing the universe to work its magic. It doesn't mean that you sit and do nothing! In terms of your goal, it may mean that each month you get closer and closer to your target, or that you reach your six month target in the first month or the last day of the six month period. Non-linear thinking and being allows for possibilities! This happens when you are in vibrational alignment with your thoughts, feelings, dreams, desires and goals.

Warning! You'll also manifest much quicker so be careful what you wish for!

Remember, your outer world is a reflection of your thoughts, feelings, energy, vibration and frequency. If you are not happy with where you are now, then congratulate yourself because your current circumstances are igniting within you the desire to create something different. And you are a creator!

So how do you lift yourself to a higher dimension, vibration and frequency?

I asked David how he gets into vibrational alignment to channel. He told me, "It's become my way of being, rather than a practice or exercise that I do. I'm never more than a few breaths away from being able to connect with higher realms. In fact, I am always connected, yet more open as a channel when I approach the experience with intent. With no intent in mind or in my heart, the experience of being connected and receiving insights is more in the realm of intuition. When I'm channeling, it is far beyond intuition since the threads of images, language, emotions and meaning that flow to me and through me are not of my creation or design. Perhaps two to three percent of my conscious awareness has any control over guiding the experience. As a channel, I receive insights and information which I then translate from the visual language, emotional and meaning threads to express or tell a story which is full of insights in alignment with my initial intention and request. I can receive information about past lives, the Akashic Records, present circumstances and future opportunities.

"In a multidimensional universe, I see this as an ability to tap into varying frequencies which hold information of value to those who are seeking beyond the borders of their 'Now' reality and their everyday experiences.

"In essence, my experience as a channel is born through an ability to release all vibrational resistance which might interfere with the purity and the clarity of the experience. That means I can always approach the heights of vibrational alignment when my heart is full of love, compassion, appreciation, gratitude and unconditional expectation for the experience to unfold in a way I have come to know to be so natural for me.

"It's like remembering the embrace of a loved one, so intimately familiar that it is possible to recall the tangible, visceral experience and relive it with every sense of being 'real,' purely through the thought and intention to connect. When I am angry, fearful or feeling alone, it is difficult to draw my attention to the feeling of being connected in a heartfelt embrace with a loved one. Yet when experiencing times of joy, elation, success or gratitude, it is far easier to sense my closeness and connection with a loved one. So too is it with channeling for me. As I imagine the feeling of being moments away from welcoming my loved one who has just returned home after some time away, the heart-full anticipation of being in their embrace can be felt in my gut as a calling, perhaps a knowing or even a yearning for the love I shall find there. So I simply imagine being welcomed into the arms of my mother and knowing only love. There is no self-doubt or lack of self-worth in my heart. Instead, I fully embrace her with all my being and that is the receptive state for me to channel. It is then that I am in the energy of perfect alignment and can allow love to flow to me and through me."

It's now time to sense your way forward into feelings and experiences that operate and lead you to a higher frequency, vibrational level and way of being; to create a beautiful shape and sound to your life!

Feelings and emotions that release vibrational resistance and lift you to a higher dimension, frequency, vibration and energy are peace, joy, love, acceptance and willingness while emotions such as anger, pride, fear, grief and apathy lower your levels of energy.

In his book, *Power vs. Force*, Dr. David R. Hawkins, MD, PhD, used a muscle testing technique from Applied Kinesiology to calibrate levels of human consciousness. Interestingly, the biggest barriers to attaining higher levels of consciousness seemed to be courage and letting go of destructive patterns of behavior.

Most people will tell you that they want to change and release old habits and destructive patterns of behavior, yet when push comes to shove, they cling to what is safe and familiar. They want to 'know before they go.' Why? Fear of the unknown, the initial discomfort that often accompanies doing something new for the first time and laziness are just some of the reasons and excuses for maintaining the status quo.

If you go to a restaurant, it's likely that you will choose from the menu a dish or food that you are familiar with or that you have had before. Be honest with me, would you choose the item that is listed on the menu as the 'mystery dish of the day?' Probably not! You'd want to know what is in it, how it is cooked, what it comes with before you order… and then it's not a mystery.

What would happen if you were to order the 'mystery dish' anyway? Maybe you won't like it and what if you did? And if you don't like it then there is nothing to stop you from ordering another dish as well!

You live in a world of infinite choice and endless opportunities, yet many people get caught up in doing the same things every single day; work routine, relationship rut, fitness habits and health regime or lack of.

Every year thousands of people across the globe attend courses and buy books on goal setting, goal getting and personal achievement. Yet they never reach their true potential or put into practice the tools and techniques that they have learned because they simply go back to the way they've always done things and choose the same food from the menu of life. As they get older, they then wonder why their life is not quite the way they imagined when they were younger. No doubt most of them settle for second best and get trapped and are lulled by complacency. They become stuck in the old patterns running at the unconscious level.

Your reality is built on your already existing store of memories, emotions, associations and identity. If you perceive only what you know, how do you ever perceive anything new?

By expanding your understanding of reality, you add new options to the list you, as a human being, carry around. To expand the boundaries of what you already know, if you want more opportunities for growth, achievement, results, you need to breakthrough and challenge old paradigms so that you say, 'I can't believe I did that,' and become more than you thought you could be. You are only ever limited by who you think you are! And now you know you are more than your thoughts.

The human potential is to grow! Growth equals life.

Just for a moment, consider a time in your life when you have created a huge shift or propelled yourself forward in some way. It could be a new career path, or venturing to a new country, opening your heart to love or to a spiritual transformation. I suspect there was an element of confusion or overwhelm just before you made that shift. You have to get used to the sense of newness, the feeling of adventurousness and the initial chaos and discomfort that happens before a shift occurs and leads you to a new way of being.

The crucial role of chaos is demonstrated in one of Swiss scientist Dr. Hans Jenny's cymatic experiments in which sound frequencies are directed into a water sample. The water vibrates as it responds to the sound and frequency creating a pattern that stays stable as long as the frequency remains the same. As the frequency changes, the stable structure and pattern goes through a short chaotic phase and then reorganizes itself into a more intricate pattern.

This is the chaos before a shift happens. For me, the chaos was the pain in my neck, for Connor it was a near-death experience. It could be an illness, the breakdown of a relationship, the loss of a dream role or career path that becomes blocked, a feeling of angst or dissatisfaction. Your reality crumbles in some way and a shift occurs. The door opens to new possibilities.

Even better, when you manifest a shift in yourself it impacts others as well. In fact, **the quickest way to bring about a shift in others is to start with yourself.** While you may think you are setting your intention to allow for something that you want, you can never set an intention in isolation, for you are not separate. When you get the new role or job, it means someone else also got a promotion or a new role. When you are in love, it means others benefit from the energy, vibration and frequency that you are emitting. When you shift it creates a whole ripple effect that impacts others that you may not previously have been aware of.

Perhaps you've heard of the 100 monkey syndrome? The story goes that back in the 1950s there was a population of Japanese monkeys on the island of Koshima. While studying these monkeys, researchers started feeding them sweet potatoes and would dump loads of them on the beach for the monkeys. The problem was that while the monkeys liked the sweet potatoes, they didn't like the sand and grit that covered them. The monkeys struggled with this problem until a young monkey dipped the sweet potato into the sea and removed the sand. This monkey then appeared to share this with other monkeys and gradually the new habit gained a following. Shortly afterwards, something remarkable happened. The number of monkeys learning this habit had reached a critical mass and every monkey on the island was washing the sweet potatoes. Not only that, but researchers reported that monkeys on other islands were doing this as well.

This is the 'morphogenic field' that biologist and author Rupert Sheldrake talks about; a force that connects each individual with all other individuals in its species, and suggests each species has a group mind. For example, if you go diving you'll see schools of fish all moving in a direction and then switching direction instantaneously as if they all got the message to switch at exactly the same moment.

For over 20 years the Transcendental Meditation organization has systematically tested, through dozens of studies, whether group meditation could reduce violence in the world. Maharishi Mahesh Yogi, the founder of Transcendental Meditation claimed that if 1% of an area had people practicing meditation, rates of shootings, crimes or even traffic accidents would go down. A study of 24 cities in the USA showed that whenever a city reached a point where 1% of the population was carrying out regular meditation, the crime rate dropped. What this all means is that the quickest way to create shifts and changes in others is to simply change yourself.

According to Dr. Hawkins, there is a second barrier to raising your consciousness and being in vibrational alignment. That barrier is 'love'. He says the reason the level of love is so difficult to achieve is sadly because our ego is so rooted in the physical domain as opposed to the spiritual domain. And I have found this to be true. Many of the people I have worked with find it challenging to love and accept themselves and so seek that love outside of themselves.

Jodie's career was booming so she was thrilled when her company asked her to relocate overseas to take up a position with greater responsibility. However, Jodie was also madly in love. Realizing that her boyfriend was in the midst of family struggles she made the decision to forego the promotion and relocation opportunity. Shortly after she left the company, the relationship came to a close and it was only then that Jodie realized that she had never spent one moment asking what she wanted. "I was so immersed in him and his needs. When I owned up to that I also came to realize how little I loved myself. That is when my healing journey truly started."

Let me ask you how you fall in love with another person? It's not a step by step process, is it?! Sometimes it's instant attraction, while other times it takes a while. The relationship may blossom over time through friendship and gradually love grows deeper. Or maybe you fall in and out of love a few times before a commitment is made.

The love you want from others is yourself calling out, 'please love me.'

So how do you fall in love with yourself? How do you get to know who you truly are? When I think back to the angst and anxiety that I used to have, it would appear that self-love is not an on-off switch. It's not a matter of 'I don't love myself and now I do,' or looking at yourself in the mirror and saying 'I love you,' when deep down you don't. Some people go on personal development programs and get results and some do not. Others read a book and sometimes they need to read the book twice before a lightbulb moment occurs. Perhaps it's a chance meeting, or a time when you are caught in the quiet. It seems to be an evolution and journey of exploring, evolving and awakening.

One of my friends, Julie-Ann Odell said, "I look at the younger version of myself with unconditional love, acceptance and intrigue. Since gaining a deeper awareness 16 years ago, I have had the courage and awareness to bless all the people and situations that I attracted back then. I hated them and resented what I had attracted until I realized the gift is knowing they were, and are, a part of what has made me who I am today. They didn't change, so I had to change myself. It was a long journey and life has been my greatest teacher. I bless all those experiences and people that were sent to my path, no matter how dark or dismal they were back then."

The biggest relationship you will ever have is the one you will have with yourself, yet so often validation and love is sought from others and through others.

It's time to remember that you are more than just your physical body. Earlier I wrote that you have an emotional, mental and spiritual body that make up your energy field. The physical systems interact with the subtle energy systems such as the meridians, the chakras and the crystalline energy systems, thus linking you with all creation. When you get out of alignment with yourself and your true life's purpose, an imbalance is initiated in your energy field, which then manifests on a physical, mental and emotional level as pain, anxiety, unhappiness and disease.

You are on the threshold of a bold step and once you take that step and start to explore, life takes on a different meaning.

Remember, in life you are both a transmitter and a receiver. Think of it like switching on the radio in your car and you hear the sounds because there is a transmitter sending the sound waves to you to receive. When you turn off the radio, the waves do not go away; it's just that you are no longer tuned into receiving them. When you receive information or have an experience, you filter the information and your experiences to give your own meaning to the information and experiences.

You are also a transmitter sending vibration, frequency and energy back out into the universe as well as being a receiver. You are not switched to on or off. You are constantly on and always transmitting and receiving.

So what is it that you want to transmit out into the world and what is it that you want to receive and bring into your world? If you are asking for the gift of healing, consider that a smile can be very healing. So smile or give someone a hug and that will start to open you to the next level. And here's a gem from Prageet Harris, who channels Alcazar (The Stargate Experience): if you seek abundance, show gratitude for any small amount that comes your way and simply add 'thank you, and bring me more.'

Like my dear soul brother, David Gross, you too are a channel learning to channel more of who you are. There is so much available to you when you make the commitment to self-love and self-development. The possibilities and potential are endless.

David Lynch, American director, author and founder of the David Lynch Foundation for Consciousness-based Education and World Peace said, "If you have a golf-ball size consciousness, when you read a book, you'll have a golf-ball size understanding, when you look out, golf-ball size awareness, and when you wake up in the morning, golf-ball size wakefulness. If you could expand that consciousness then when you read the book you'll have more understanding, more awareness when you look out, and when you wake up, more wakefulness."

When you understand that you are pure energy there are endless possibilities to change your reality and shatter your beliefs of who you truly are. And when you do, you have the opportunity to tap into your divine genius. After all, your true purpose, and to feel purposeful is to simply evolve and expand your wakefulness, awareness and consciousness!

May you and your life be the reflection of your perfection of the connection to all that you truly are!

Spirals

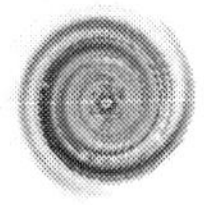

Everything is built on shapes and patterns including yourself and the life you have created for yourself. Sacred Geometry gives you a visual representation to see the beauty and possibilities of your own evolution. You can either remain static in your life, confined by the boundaries, fears, patterns and beliefs you have placed around yourself or, as more information becomes available, you can expand.

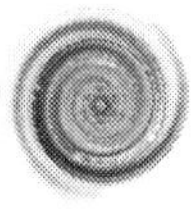

Sacred Geometry allows you to fully consider your creative abilities as the shapes intertwine, expand inwards and outwards from the simple to the complex as you connect your physical, mental and emotional bodies.

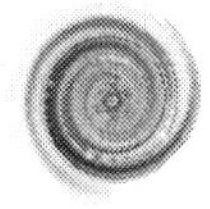

Everything in your universe is made up of energy that is constantly flowing and changing form all the time, including YOU. That means you are entangled and connected to everything around you. How you behave, how you think and feel, and what you say is also vibrating into this field of energy. Your vibration and positive energy can and does affect and impact others.

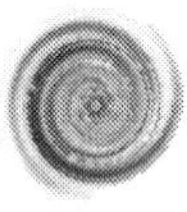

When you hear sound, you are hearing energy. When you create sounds you are transmitting energy. Sound affects how matter itself vibrates and can change how matter vibrates. That would mean that it can affect how YOU vibrate. And your life is in harmony with the vibration and frequency you are sending out.

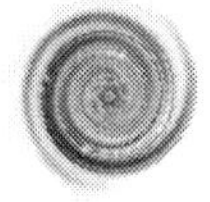

Your current reality is built on your already existing store of memories, emotions, associations and identity. You are only ever limited by who you think you are! And you are more than your thoughts. You are also a transmitter

sending vibration, frequency and energy back out into the universe as well as a receiver. You are constantly on and always transmitting and receiving.

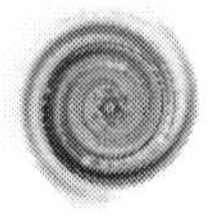

A morphogenic field connects each individual with all other individuals which means that when you manifest a shift in yourself it impacts others as well.

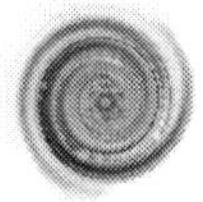

The biggest relationship you will ever have is the one you will have with yourself. When you understand that you are pure energy, there are endless possibilities to change your reality and shatter your beliefs of who you truly are.

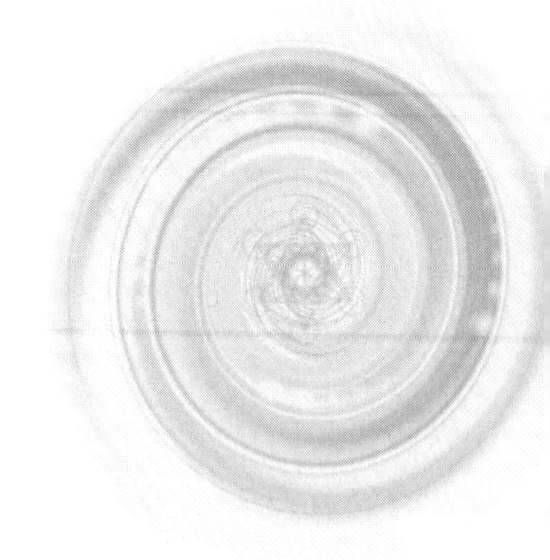

The Journey Continues...

"When you are no longer able to change a situation, you are challenged to change yourself."

Carol Talbot

I am not interested in a life of 'blah' and mediocrity. There is always more to discover and I am committed to a constant journey of experiences which offer opportunities to ignite and engage myself and others in the evolution of a different perspective.

My imagination leads me towards the development of a device that can actually measure and give you a visual representation of your predominant vibration and frequency, and how to increase your vibration and frequency. It could be a little like those wrist bands that tell you how many steps you've taken each day or registers your sleep patterns. Where is your imagination leading you?

When you shatter your beliefs about reality and realize who you truly are, then you can step into a new way of being. And if you are curious and ready to expand your awareness, your consciousness, your heart and mind, to step into a fuller focus of who you are, then you only have to look at the image of the spiral that has been used throughout this first book. A spiral represents constant and ongoing evolution with no end.

As your life expands and evolves, keep asking... what is next?

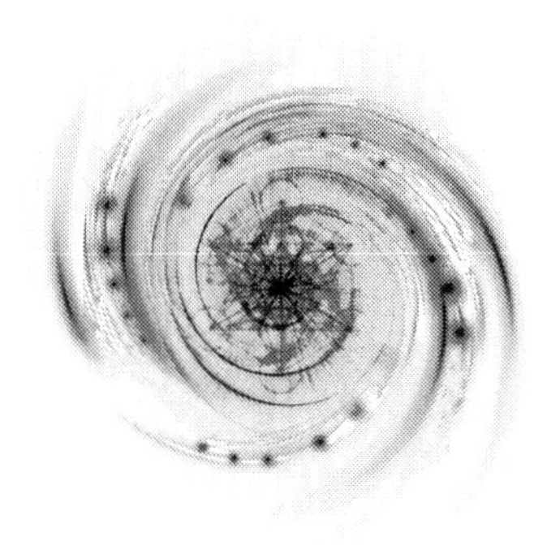

References & Resources

Chapter One

Mihaly Csikszentmihalyi – *Flow*

Morris Massey – *The People Puzzle*

Dr. Bruce Lipton – *The Biology of a Belief*

Chapter Two

Global Mentoring Walk – *www.vitalvoices.org*

Chapter Four

HeartMath Institute – *www.heartmath.org*

Nels Quevli – *Cell Intelligence: The Cause of Growth, Heredity, and Instinctive Actions*

Chapter Five

Sri Aurobindo – *www.aurosociety.org*

Maharishi University – *www.mum.edu*

Chapter Six

David Suzuki, *The Nature of Things* – *www.cbc.ca/natureofthings*

Chapter Seven

Mas Sajady – *www.mas-sajady.com*

Eben Alexander – *Proof of Heaven*

Chapter Eight

Carlos Castaneda – *www.cleargreen.com*
Michelle Karen – *www.michellekaren.com*
Hemi Sync – *www.hemi-syn.com*
Holosync – *www.centerpointe.com*
Dolores Cannon (QHHT) – *www.qhhtofficial.com*
Michael Newton – *www.newtoninstitute.org*
Brian Weiss – *www.brianweiss.com*
Alexandra Salkova McKenzie – *www.innerselfconsultancy.com*
Robert Schwartz – *Your Soul's Plan and Your Soul's Gifts*
Jim B. Tucker – *Return to Life: Extraordinary Cases of Children Who Remember Past Lives*

Chapter Ten

Pachamama Alliance – *www.pachamama.org*
Kambo – *www.iakp.org*

Chapter Eleven

Drunvalo Melchizedek – *www.drunvalo.net*

Chapter Twelve

Villas Xichu – *www.villas-xichu.com*
Christina Sol – *www.ayahuascapalomablanca.com*
Master Zhou – *www.masterzhou.com*
Cymatics – *www.cymatics.org*
Dr. Masaru Emoto – *www.masaru-emoto.net*
Zoe Henderson – *www.intuitivehealer-horsewhisperer.com*

Chapter Thirteen

David Gross – *www.anewwayofbeing.com*
Dr. David R. Hawkins – *Power vs. Force*
The Stargate Experience – *www.thestargateexperience.com*

About the Author

Carol has a rare ability to see a deeper perspective within each and every individual allowing her to create a blueprint of action steps to move you forward. This makes the process of growth and expansion an easier and more joyful journey. Known as the NLP (neuro linguistic programming) expert in the Middle East, and an NLP Master Trainer, Carol utilizes its many tools and techniques to create rapid shifts for groups and individuals as well as breakthrough experiences including one of mankind's older change promoting tools, the fire-walk.

Carol has guided and inspired people around the globe, offering motivating events for world class companies. The response to Carol as a motivational and subject matter speaker at conferences, events or workshops is always the same... 'WOW!'

As a seeker, searcher, learner and explorer Carol has experienced many of the indigenous medicines with tribes in Ecuador, Peru and Mexico and the depth of insight that they gift us with. Her travels and curious nature have led her to a desire to bring YOU an opportunity to move in a direction that maybe you've not gone before. An opportunity to expand your awareness, your consciousness, your heart and mind to step into a fuller focus of who YOU are.

www.caroltalbot.me **www.youthedivinegenius.com**

Printed in Great Britain
by Amazon